Raymond Radiguet

Twayne's World Authors Series
French Literature

David O'Connell, Editor
University of Illinois

TWAS 725

RAYMOND RADIGUET (1923)
Photograph by Man Ray
Courtesy of M. René Radiguet

Raymond Radiguet

By James P. McNab

Guilford College

Twayne Publishers • Boston

Raymond Radiguet

James P. McNab

Copyright © 1984 by G. K. Hall & Company
All Rights Reserved
Published by Twayne Publishers
A Division of G. K. Hall & Company
70 Lincoln Street
Boston, Massachusetts 02111

Book Production by Elizabeth Todesco

Book Design by Barbara Anderson

Printed on permanent/durable acid-free
paper and bound in the United States of
America.

**Library of Congress Cataloging in
Publication Data**

McNab, James P.
  Raymond Radiguet.

  (Twayne's world authors series; TWAS 725)
  Bibliography: p. 158
  Includes index.
  1. Radiguet, Raymond, 1903–1923—
Criticism and interpretation.
I. Title. II. Series.
PQ2635.A25Z72 1984   843'.912   84–10893
ISBN 0–8057–6572–7

Contents

About the Author

Born in Falkirk, Scotland, James P. McNab is Dana Professor of French and Chairman of Foreign Languages at Guilford College, Greensboro, North Carolina. He is a graduate (M.A. Hons. in French with German) of the University of Edinburgh, and of Duke University (M.A. and Ph.D. in French). He held a James B. Duke scholarship to Duke, where his doctoral dissertation on Jean Cocteau was directed by Wallace Fowlie. He is Associate Editor of the journal *Degré Second: Studies in French Literature*, and was Romance Editor of *Semasia: Beiträge zur germanisch-romanischen Sprachforschung*. His articles on Cocteau, Mauriac, Radiguet, and on nineteenth-century French poetry have appeared in *French Review, Hartford Studies in Literature, French Literature Series* (University of South Carolina), *Philological Papers* (University of West Virgina), and *Guilford Review*. Before assuming his position at Guilford College, he was Associate Professor and Head of Foreign Languages at Virginia Polytechnic Institute and State University. His current research is in French literary trends of the 1920s.

Preface

Raymond Radiguet died at the age of twenty, in 1923, leaving a substantial body of work, much of it little known even in France, and quite unknown abroad. To be sure, his two novels, *Le Diable au corps (Devil in the Flesh)* and *Le Bal du comte d'Orgel (Ball at Count d'Orgel's)*, published in 1923 and 1924, respectively, are widely read. On the other hand, his poetry, including even *Les Joues en feu (Cheeks on Fire)*, which appeared in 1925, has captured a small audience. The large number of short critical pieces Radiguet published in his lifetime, or those that have come out posthumously, have attracted little attention in France, and practically none outside the country. This is understandable for a number of reasons, but it is to be regretted. Radiguet's work, fragmentary though it is in many places, reveals extraordinary talent. Without exception, those who knew him considered his intelligence and creative talents exceptional. Some had no hesitation in calling him a genius. Moreover, Radiguet was in the right place—Paris—at the right time—around 1920—to be exposed to and to observe other gifted artists. He numbered among his friends, at various times, André Salmon, Max Jacob, André Breton, Tristan Tzara, Pierre Reyerdy, the painter Juan Gris, the sculptor Constantin Brancusi, the composers Georges Auric and Darius Milhaud, and above all Jean Cocteau, of many talents.

A major problem in trying to approach Radiguet's work and life is that they are so closely intertwined with the career of Jean Cocteau. While Radiguet was alive, Cocteau was extraordinarily close to him, as intimate friend, protector, and indeed impresario. Radiguet's death left the older man disconsolate, but determined to erect a myth around his protégé's brief life. Cocteau spared no effort to enhance Radiguet's reputation, to clothe the simple facts of his existence in the mantle of legend, and to give to them the appearance of having run a divinely inspired, preordained course. His retelling of this life went from an anodyne affirmation that he slipped off gently into death—whereas he died alone and in terror—to what amounts to a major revision of *Le Bal du comte d'Orgel*, and a major part in other works by Radiguet. In view of the leading role played by Cocteau in Radiguet's evolution, and the vital earlier influences on him, the present study devotes a large chapter to Radiguet's life, in an attempt to extricate the writer—to the extent this is possible—from the forces around him that shaped his talent, and from the legend carefully created by Cocteau.

The first full-length study of Radiguet's poetry, by David Noakes, appeared in 1952. While excellent, it is still the only one, and many of Radiguet's carefully wrought poems have never been explicated. The second chapter of the present work charts the evolution of Radiguet the poet from ready acceptance of the avant-garde to a conservative, traditional posture, through an analysis of many of his poems in chronological order.

The two chapters devoted to Radiguet's novels require no justification, in view of the sound reputation they have enjoyed with both critic and reading public alike. It is noteworthy however that in his prose fiction as in his other endeavors Radiguet's attempt to "find himself" as artist led him to a degree of conservatism that has not been properly recognized up to now.

With the appearance of Radiguet's *Oeuvres Complètes* (Complete works), edited by Simone Lamblin (Paris: Club des Libraires de France, 1959), a more accurate idea of the range of Radiguet's writing was given for the first time. Certainly, these two volumes are not truly complete, but they made available not just poems that had either been scattered in various small collections, in ephemeral journals, or had not been published at all, but also a large number of critical articles that had suffered a similar fate. Drawing upon this edition, on the numerous critical articles, which are still largely unknown, chapter 5 traces the evolution of Radiguet's ideas on life and art. Many of the pieces are brief; others are tantalizingly incomplete. Nonetheless here too the picture that emerges is quite coherent, of a writer moving rather consistently to a conservative, perhaps even reactionary aesthetic stance.

Without the support of a number of individuals, it would have been impossible for me to complete this study. In the first place it is a privilege to name M. René Radiguet for his encouragement, and for his kindness in allowing me to quote quite extensively from his brother's work. I owe a debt of gratitude to Wallace Fowlie, who channeled my budding interest in Radiguet. With gratitude I also acknowledge the support provided by two small grants from

Virginia Polytechnic Institute and State University, which allowed me to examine journals of Radiguet's time, necessary to an understanding of both author and period.

James P. McNab

Guilford College

Chronology

1903   Raymond Radiguet born June 18 in Parc Saint-Maur, a small town on the eastern outskirts of Paris. The oldest of seven children.

1909   Enters the local grade school, Saint-Maur Centre.

1913   Admitted to the Lycée Charlemagne, in the Bastille district of Paris, for secondary studies.

1914   With outbreak of World War I, frequently plays truant, reads books on his father's little boat anchored in the Marne River.

1917   In April, meets Alice, a soldier's wife, with whom he has an affair. She becomes inspiration for Marthe in *Devil in the Flesh*.

1918   ·Leaves the Lycée Charlemagne to try his luck as writer and illustrator. Publishes first piece, "Galanterie Française," in *Le Canard Enchaîné*. Meets the writer-editor André Salmon, who assigns him work and puts him in touch with the poet Max Jacob and other artists. Beginning of his friendship with Jacob, and with Jean Cocteau. His talent is appreciated by André Breton, who vies with Cocteau as an influence on his development. Writing under name Raimon Rajky, he publishes poems in *L'Eveil, L'Heure,* and *Sic*. Sends poems to Apollinaire, who, indignant at what he considers a pastiche of his own work, does not answer.

1919   Corresponds with Tristan Tzara, the founder of Dada, and begins writing for Breton's journal *Littérature*. Starts work on the novel *Devil in the Flesh,* completes two manuscript collections of poetry, *Le Bonnet d'âne* (The dunce's cap) and *Couleurs sans danger* (Harmess colors). Begins writing articles and poems for the manuscript collector Jacques Doucet.

1920   Having broken with Breton, collaborates with Cocteau in creating the avant-garde broadsheet *Le Coq*. Writes the comic opera *Paul et Virginie* in collaboration with Cocteau; it is not performed because Erik Satie does not write the music as anticipated. Writes for *Ecrits Nouveaux* and *Action*. Regularly attends Saturday-night dinners with the "Mutual Admiration Society" (made up of Cocteau and his artist friends). Publication of a first *Joues en feu (Cheeks on Fire)*, poems. Writes *Les Pélican*, a play in two acts.

1921   Writes short story *Denise* while on holiday in Carqueiranne, near Toulon. Publishes *Devoirs de vacances* (Summer assignments), poems, illustrated by Irène Lagut. Spends summer at Le Piqueÿ, on the bay of Arcachon, with friends Cocteau, Jean and Valentine Hugo (both painters, he was geat-grandson of Victor Hugo), and others, working on *Devil in the Flesh*. Publication and performance of *Les Pélican*. 1921–22, love affair with Englishwoman Beatrice Hastings, who had been Modigliani's mistress. Writes for *Le Gaulois*.

1922   Publishes articles and poems in *L'Oeuf dur, Les Feuilles Libres, Catalogue*. On impulse, runs off to Corsica with the sculptor Brancusi; chafing at Cocteau's constant presence. Regular customer of the bar *Le Boeuf sur le toit* (The ox on the roof), a legendary meeting-place for artists in Paris. Begins drinking heavily. In summer, in the company of Cocteau, in the Lavandou and nearby Pramousquier, writes much of the novel *Count d'Orgel*. He and Cocteau put in appearance at funeral of Marcel Proust.

1923   Continues drinking heavily. Visits England (London, Harrow, Oxford) with Cocteau. Received there by Reginald Bridgeman, private secretary to British Ambassador in Paris. Publication of *Devil in the Flesh* by Grasset, accompanied by a publicity barrage. It wins the newly created New World Prize. Attends fashionable balls given by the comte Etienne de Beaumont and by the couturier Paul Poiret. During the summer at Le Piqueÿ, corrects the proofs of *Count d'Orgel*. Works on long essay on his native province, "Ile-de-France, Ile d'Amour." This unfinished work was to be a long appendix to *Devil in the Flesh*. Does research for fictional biography of the fifteenth-century nobleman and poet Charles d'Orléans. It is never written. Returns to Paris October, feeling sick. Grasset obtains a deferment from army to allow him to correct proofs of *Count d'Orgel*. Settles in Hotel Foyot (near the Luxembourg Palace) with Bronya Perlmutter, far from Cocteau. Life of dissipation and increasing sickness. December 12, dies of typhoid, probably induced by eating infected oysters at Le Piqueÿ; dies alone, in clinic in the rue Piccini in Paris. Gabrielle "Coco" Chanel arranges funeral, and burial in Père-Lachaise. Cocteau absent from funeral.

1924   In July, publication of *Count d'Orgel*, after extensive correction of proofs by Cocteau and the writer Joseph Kessel.

1925   Publication of the definitive *Joues en feu*, a collection of thirty-four poems.

Chapter One

Raymond Radiguet: The Life

The image we have of Raymond Radiguet is of necessity arrested by his early death. His lifespan was little more than that of a child. However, in the words of François Mauriac, "that child was a master,"[1] of "a lucidity without equal at so early an age."[2] According to Mauriac—and this assessment was shared by all those who knew Radiguet—the youth displayed extraordinary maturity, possessing the ability to see clearly into the hearts of others, revealing even what they did not see: "Radiguet shows us, through glass, the workings of hearts entirely engaged in deceiving themselves."[3]

In complete contrast to the volubility of Jean Cocteau, it was Radiguet's reserve and taciturnity that struck those who knew him. He was frugal of word and gesture, attentive, observant, and intent, as though he wished to lose no part of what he saw or heard. It is paradoxical that, nearsighted as he was, his powers of observation were remarkable. To some extent, these qualities are characteristic of a tradition of French writing: the moralists, especially those of the seventeenth and eighteenth centuries, whom Radiguet knew well. But his intense power of concentration and his lucidity, combined with some secrecy, a certain lack of spontaneity, and a rather deep-seated skepticism, derive to a greater degree from the circumstances in which he was raised.

Radiguet and the Marne

Forming a backdrop to much of what he wrote is that part of the province of Ile-de-France immediately to the southeast of Paris and dominated by the Marne River. Certainly, although Radiguet was born just six miles or so from the heart of Paris, in the little town of Parc Saint-Maur, it is the Marne and not the capital that fills his vision of the region. In his writing it is represented as a peaceful body of water, a cradle of renewal in time of stress, a source of consolation, and a refuge. In a long, unfinished essay entitled "Ile-de-France, Ile d'Amour" (Ile-de France, island of love), Radiguet celebrates his love for his native province, and in particular for the river, viewed preeminently as a place of tranquillity.[4] He contrasts its gentleness with the bleak Seine, of which it is a tributary. For Radiguet, the Seine is beautiful only where it crosses Paris. Afterwards, on its way to Normandy, it becomes dismal again.

By and large, Radiguet chooses not to talk about the Marne as the place of pleasure—dancing establishments, bars, restaurants—that was very popular with the Parisians throughout the first part of the century. In "Ile-de-France, Ile d'Amour" he does describe his fascination as a child with Nogent-sur-Marne, the pleasure-seeker's center, a quintessential symbol of the *Belle Epoque,* its skating rink, its halls where couples danced the tango, and where fights would break out, then to be reported in the Monday-morning newspaper.[5] He hastens to add, however, that his personal acquaintance with the Marne is quite dissimilar: "But that Marne was not mine. And I scarcely knew Nogent except through newspaper articles. As for the walks that almost every Sunday I and my brothers took accompanied by my father, out steps were never headed in that direction. It was a calmer Marne that we would walk alongside most of the time, toward La Varenne."[6]

Nor was "his" Marne the region made famous by the events of World War I at the very time that Radiguet was living there. It was in the Marne that two of the most famous battles of the conflict were fought. In the first, General Joffre turned back the German army commanded by von Moltke and ensured the safety of Paris from 1914 on. In the second, General Joffre and the Allied armies turned back the Germans in the summer of 1918 and continued a counteroffensive that culminated eventually in the defeat of the enemy. The war is by no means absent from Radiguet's work. Its chronology determines the events of his novel *Devil in the Flesh,* as a background imperative. As a boy, he would cross the river to visit the train station of Champigny, through which all the military trains would pass, heading for the front to the east, or bringing back the many thousands of wounded. Radiguet remembered these troop movements. He did briefly celebrate in writing[7] the victories of the Marne. But by and large the Marne of which he writes is not that of heroism, victory, and patriotism.

Whereas Cocteau wrote some surprisingly bombastic—and largely unknown—war poetry,[8] Radiguet's posture here, as in all circumstances, was of relative detachment, distance, or coolness. He had a natural preference for litotes over hyperbole, irony over involvement, and this is reflected in a tranquil, understated view of the Marne. He did identify closely with his region, and in turn identified it as part of the larger province of Ile-de-France. He was very conscious of its history as having begun long before 1914, and refused to be swept along (unlike Cocteau) by current events and passions. He mentioned among the region's claims to distinction the presence there in the seventeenth century of the novelist Mme de Lafayette, who became an inspiration for him, as well as the eighteenth-century painter Watteau, whom Radiguet admired and who made Nogent-sur-Marne his home. It is not an exaggeration to state that Radiguet consistently deflected attention away from the specific, precise details of his own childhood—the facts, in other words—and replaced them by a more poetic myth of happy days spent in a large Franch garden.

Radiguet describes his childhood in rather idyllic terms, as uneventful years spent in the country, beside the river, which flowed through verdant meadows, gentle landscapes, and alongside orchards. Although the banks of the Marne were pleasant, and to a large extent still are, Radiguet exaggerated the rusticity of this setting, which was almost a suburb of the capital. In like fashion, he transforms the penury of his childhood into a privilege, a positive advantage and virtue. The overall image that results is quite poetic but not, perhaps, true to life:

How mediocre a childhood spent in the midst of wealth is likely to be! And, for a well-formed heart, in which envy can find no place, how great are its pleasures when they are numbered, and must come from oneself alone! I would not exchange my memories for those of anyone else. That childhood, as flat as a lawn, which, for eleven years, stretches as far as the eye can see, unimpeded by any irregular feature, how I now love to frolic and luxuriate in it! These rank weeds in which I would run, imagining I was free . . . I remember the plot of land in the avenue des Rochers adjoining the house of my very first years. My memories! Like the weeds I see them standing at different heights. There are some taller than I am, whereas there are others that my foot threatens to crush. ("Ile-de-France, Ile d'Amour," 329–30)

It is customary to consider Radiguet one of the leaders of the return to "classicism" in the immediate postwar years, and it may be that his reserve, his sober writing style, and his natural aversion for the confessional mode derive from this "classicism." Such an assessment, however, probably puts the cart before the horse. In all likelihood, Radiguet wished to conceal a number of aspects of his upbringing, and it is rather this desire to direct attention away from himself and much of his background that played a major part in his adoption of "classicism." Happy to identify with the Marne in the Ile-de-France, this cradle of French literature and civilization, he was equally happy to leave behind and forget the particular, local, existential circumstances of a childhood spent in the relatively unattractive town of Parc Saint-Maur.

Childhood: Family and School

Raymond Radiguet was born in Parc Saint-Maur on June 18, 1903, the oldest of seven children. His father, Jules-Maurice, eked out an existence as a cartoonist. He had been one of the associates of the *Chat Noir* (The Black Cat), a very famous artistic cabaret in Montmartre, at the close of the nineteenth century. Among its collaborators were the writers Mac-Nab and Alphonse Allais and the cartoonist Caran d'Ache. Maurice Radiguet submitted his drawings to a number of Parisian newspapers. In the course of the war, he made drawings for a number of anti-German albums in a series entitled, none too subtly, *Kolossâle Kollection.*[9] What they lack in refinement, they make up for in vitality.

Maurice Radiguet was some eighteen years older than his wife. Caught up in the need to earn his living, commuting on an almost daily basis to Paris to place his drawings, he appears to have left Raymond considerable freedom, especially after the outbreak of hostilities. Before the war, however, he did take an active interest in Raymond's studies. In the primary school in Parc Saint-Maur, which he attended from 1909 until 1913, Raymond was a good student. In the absence of a local *lycée,* he then attended classes at the *lycée* Charlemagne, in the vicinity of the place de la Bastille, in the east of Paris. While his innate intelligence was unquestioned, his school record was far from brilliant, since he increasingly played truant. His father took him out of school and set about teaching him Latin and Greek himself. This was not very effective. Raymond continued to miss classes and read his favorite authors on a boat—his father's—anchored on the Marne. He read voraciously and borrowed large numbers of books—in particular the French classics—from his father's library. School as such had little appeal for him, and at the age of fifteen he left school, in order to try to earn some money while carving out a career for himself with his drawing and writing.

Maurice Radiguet was well placed to know about the pleasures and dangers of life in Paris, and he came to be unhappy about the fast-paced life that Cocteau eventually showed his son. However, the tone of letters written by Radiguet to his father remained affectionate. As soon as he was able, he sent money home to help out. For his part, Maurice did not appear to hold Raymond's friends responsible for his untimely death. He wrote to the composer Francis Poulenc in 1924: "If, later on, you could give me, either in a group shot or separately portraits of those who were, these last years, his best friends: you, Cocteau, two or three others that you know better than I, I could not describe the joy I would feel. Of all of you he spoke to me with such affection . . . ."[10] In sum, relations between father and son were without doubt strained on many occasions, but a close bond of love or affection was never broken. Maurice Radiguet himself summed up their relationship by saying that a wall did often separate them, "but the wall was not very solid. A good, affectionate push would bring it tumbling down."[11]

Whereas Maurice Radiguet was descended from the family of Mme de Pompadour, the favorite of King Louis XV in the eighteenth century, his wife, Jeanne-Louise-Marie Tournier, sprang from an equally celebrated but more distinguished family. She was apparently a descendant of Josephine Tascher, the noble Creole from Martinique, who married first the vicomte de Beauharnais, and then, of course, Napoleon Bonaparte. Cocteau celebrated his young friend's ancestry in a poem of which one quatrain reads:

> Let us not be surprised if your refined strength
> Adds to the black laurel the roses of love.
> For you combine within you the blood of Josephine
> And that of the Pompadour.[12]

A bride almost as soon as she left the local grade school, she spent most of her time seeing to Radiguet's brothers and sisters: after Raymond came three of each. In response to a question about his mother, Radiguet is said to have replied: "I do not know. I never see her face. She is always bent over, doing up the shoe-laces of one of my brothers or sisters."[13] The sheer number of younger children probably made it inevitable that Radiguet should feel cut off from contact with his mother. The range of ages, moreover, was such that his mother, living in relative poverty, without much help, simply could not pay attention to her oldest. There is affection in a typical conclusion to a letter that Radiguet wrote to his parents; but there is also irony in his reference to a newborn brother whom he has not yet seen: "I embrace both of you, as well as all the children, including the brother I have not yet met. Raymond."[14] Such considerations would not perhaps be important if they did not have a bearing upon Radiguet's early departure from home, his decision to be a writer, and the direction that his writing followed, as well as a certain tendency toward self-destruction. But it seems clear they did.

Memory: The Response to Childhood

In looking back over his childhood, Radiguet saw largely an unruffled surface, years of relative tranquillity. He did discern, however, a few moments or incidents that stood out and struck him as being particularly significant. His very earliest memory, described in "Ile-de-France, Ile d'Amour," went back to the age of two: "I see myself . . . led by my nurse every morning to the girls' boarding school from which my mother had graduated four years earlier. The gentle feel of the warm knees and breasts is something I have never been able to recover in the way in which I experienced it then. I felt these caresses so different from those of my mother or of my nurse" ("Ile-de-France, Ile d'Amour," 330).

Without wishing to make too much of this scene, one may nonetheless suggest its importance. In the first place the sensuality that it translates would be a constant in Radiguet's life and work. But there is also an indication here of a lack of satisfaction at the same time that there is an emphasis on sensuality. Apparently the child did not find at home the warmth he craved. And in seeking it elsewhere, later, he was not able to find it. It is a small, further sign of Radiguet's sense of being disaffected or of "not belonging."

Two other incidents are remembered with particular clarity as being grave, momentous, or solemn features in the relatively featureless landscape of his childhood. Both involve death, and neither takes place in his home. They are described in "Ile-de-France, Ile d'Amour." In the first, when Radiguet was ten, he witnessed the suicide of a housemaid who threw herself from the roof of her employers'—the Radiguets' neighbors'—house. The second involved an engaged couple on a swing in a park on the island known as the Island of Love, adjacent to Ormesson, just downriver from Saint-Maur. Radiguet was walking back from Ormesson with his father when his gaze was drawn by the sight of the two, swinging ever higher, in defiance of the regulation that only one person at a time was allowed on the swing. At first the boy was attracted by the sexual suggestiveness of the scene, the young man's taking the swing higher and higher, the young woman's laughter, a glimpse of her thighs, the squeak of the swing, like that of bedsprings. Here, as elsewhere, Radiguet has a natural affinity for presenting scenes very reminiscent of paintings by French rococo artists: in this instance, *The Swing* (1769) by Fragonard.[15] But whereas a sense of foreboding remains latent in the paintings of Watteau, Boucher, or Fragonard, the misfortune actually takes place in Radiguet's work. Here, it is a measure of Radiguet's precocity—he was scarcely eleven when this scene took place in June 1914—that he should have registered with such clarity the full import of what took place, and be able to recall it so effectively eight or nine years later. As the young man drove the swing higher and higher, the girl's laughter became shrill, grating. Suddenly she screamed. The swing was almost vertical in relation to the crossbeam, but the boy was alone. The girl lay on the ground in her white dress, lifeless, with blood gushing from her throat. Her fiancé could not at first come down, borne along by the movement of the swing. Radiguet saw in this event something awesome, worthy of Greek tragedy, "an atrocious spectacle" that impressed him "like one of these savage ceremonies of antiquity" ("Ile-de-France, Ile d'Amour," 331–32).

Both of these memories, the suicide of the housemaid and the death of the girl on the swing, were used as incidents in *Devil in the Flesh.* In Radiguet's estimation, both carried a message and a meaning. He interpreted the death of the housemaid as a premonitory event, heralding the imminent outbreak of World War I. He believed that the accident involving the swing was somehow a warning that fate can step unbidden into life and change its direction. Both events are superficially banal. But, as they are depicted by Radiguet, they appear profoundly meaningful. Indeed they could be compared to what Baudelaire, in his prose poems, called a "solemnity."

Baudelaire was very conscious of the apparent disappearance of meaning from the modern world. The nocturnal city scenes of his poetry, often grotesque, uncanny, or sinister, reflect this pessimism. A part of Baudelaire's response to this flight of meaning was an intense scrutiny and interrogation of encounters and incidents to which he was witness. He called such scenes, which appeared insignificant but in fact were profoundly meaningful and revelatory for him, "solemnities."[16] Like Baudelaire and the symbolists before him, and the surrealists who were his contemporaries, but independently of both, Radiguet sought meaning in the banal occurrence.

There is in Radiguet's work no proof that he started out with a ready-made, cohesive canon of values and beliefs. There is especially no sign that religion played any part in his upbringing. Religion is absent from his writing. On the other hand, there is a low-keyed but quite consistent emphasis on the reality of fate. And a means of understanding fate is provided by the intrusion into life of seemingly mundane events that one might call, borrowing Baudelaire's term, "solemnities": grave relations of meaning to be read into incidents, difficult to decipher and communicate, but no less important for that.

Radiguet's remembrance of these two events from his childhood appears, therefore, a little discordant within the context of the impression he tries to give elsewhere of a happy childhood. It is just one of a number of anomalous elements to be detected in any analysis of Radiguet's childhood as he describes it. The first, most striking of these is the fact that he almost never presents an interior, domestic scene in his autobiographical writing. It is rather surprising that we find only scant description of his house, barely a mention of his mother, infrequent evocation of his six younger brothers and sisters, with almost no mention of them as individuals, as opposed to lumping them together as a group. One finds virtually no descriptions of family celebrations, such as birthdays or Christmas, spent together. There is only a hint of the indubitably difficult material circumstances in which Radiguet lived with his family. We know, however, from his later correspondence that he helped out financially just as soon as he was able. It is no exaggeration, either, to say that in his writings personal communications are generally difficult, there are frequent misunderstandings between spouses and lovers and between parents and children.

There is a curious ambiguity also in Radiguet's description of his native town, Parc Saint-Maur: "We lived in Parc Saint-Maur. I had been born there, I had never left it, an animal in a park, so much so that this word park was accurate for me. I walked about it like a deer in a park, without for a moment thinking myself a prisoner and sighing for freedom. On the contrary I was proud of my native town" ("Ile-de-France, Ile d'Amour," 327). This affirmation, that he was quite happy to be in Parc Saint-Maur, without having any possibility of leaving it, sounds oddly like the statement of someone who makes the best out of a bad situation. In point of fact, just as soon as he could leave, he did. At the age of fifteen or sixteen, when he was afforded the opportunity, by friends, to spend the night in Paris instead of returning home, he did so.

From a very early age, Radiguet appears to have been endowed with the ability to observe and sum up a situation. This gift for analysis involved him in a constant act of appraisal, measurement, and calculation. When he first left Parc Saint-Maur for Paris, his new literary acquaintances remarked upon his shyness. But before long he was conversant with this new milieu and the reaction he provoked was astonishment that one so young could be so mature. He knew how to assess or "read" a situation and take advantage of it. This precocity was not without an element of sadness in the eyes of some observers: "He was a child without youthfulness, without exuberance, without illusions. He reminded me of these young Chinese scholars who at twenty, wear upon their ageless mask the imprint of premature old age."[17] Radiguet himself was aware of his precocity, but, eager to outstrip childhood as quickly as possible, and leave it behind him, he hated to be considered a child prodigy or to be praised as such. In Cocteau's words, "He liked the idea of getting older. He hated youth in a Wildean sense of the term. He dreaded its charm and dazzle. Where others say 'When I was young,' he would say: 'When I am older.' He awaited that moment when his spirit and his physique would be in harmony."[18]

Radiguet has often been compared to another child prodigy, Rimbaud, and this comparison is inevitable, since each composed all of his works at an astonishingly early age. But there is a fundamental difference between the two. Very early, Rimbaud recognized enemies in his childhood, individuals and institutions against which he revolted with violence. Distaste, anger, and a sense of injustice underlie many of his poems. Church and priest and pro-

vincial ugliness come under attack in "First Communions," while
in "Seven-Year Old Poets" the smug mother is viewed with loathing,
as the enemy.[19] Rimbaud condemns even his ancestors, whose "bad
blood" courses in his veins.[20] Rimbaud's poetry, composed between
the ages of sixteen and nineteen, grew out of adolescent indignation
and revolt, fueled by hatred and the need for freedom. Radiguet's
work was written between the ages of fifteen and twenty. But
Radiguet understood the limitations that hedged his early years,
lived within them, and tried to select from the situation whatever
could be usefully salvaged. Rather than revolt pointlessly against a
constricted life in a crowded house where he was but one child
among many, in a small town that was little more than a dormitory
suburb of Paris, the oldest son accepted these facts, put up with
them, and then tried to retrieve from the circumstances whatever
positive features he could. Rimbaud appears to have revolted against
what he perceived as the tyranny of life at home. Radiguet on the
other hand suffered from less concrete adversity: a sense of being
just one more child among many in a shabby setting. His response,
in his writing, was to give his house, his town, and his family
rather short shrift, while embracing the larger background to his
life—the Marne and the Ile-de-France—about which he need feel
no sense of embarrassment, humiliation, or deprivation.

Radiguet's accommodation to reality was purchased at considerable cost in human terms. His characteristic position was that of
someone on the outside looking in or looking on, often with dis-
approval: "All those who knew Radiguet tell us of a small, nearsighted person, habitually silent, who would cast his marble gaze
upon the conversations and the laughter."[21] Although he was not
without friends—he exercised considerable charm upon those with
whom he came in contact—a final impression we have of him is of
loneliness. This is true of his early childhood; he suggests it in some
brief, schematic notes entitled *Souvenirs d'enfance* (Memories of childhood), where he recalls the street on which he lived: "Avenue du
Rocher—tricycle in the garden—the garden—cherry-tree on a
mound—for me a mountain—an adjacent field, grass three times
taller than I, where you can hide—I hide by myself—having no
playmate"[22] And it is even true of his death. He had many friends
in Paris; but, by a chance that appears appropriate to his condition,
he died alone, shortly before dawn, with no one to ease his last
moments.

Lurking beneath Radiguet's quite disdainful appearance of self-assurance was another, obverse aspect to him. The dangers awaiting a young man in Paris in 1918 were as prodigious as the rewards. The "bizarre celebrations and fashions"[23] that one critic has described were espoused by Radiguet. Paris was not, in this postwar period, conducive to the preservation of life or the conservation of human energy. But Radiguet threw himself into that maelstrom of parties, alcohol, and eventually drugs with particularly reckless abandon. It would not be too extreme to suggest the existence within him of a self-destructive urge, a suicidal tendency. It seems clear that his early deprivation and dissatisfaction, leading to a doubt about his own worth, conditioned this as much as his more positive qualities.

In his human contacts, Radiguet displayed the same analytical talents he brought to bear on most life situations. This was true of his relations with women, for even here he continued to examine and scrutinize the relationship, and of his association with Jean Cocteau. He conveyed a rather disquieting impression of being very lucid, like a presiding judge about to hand down a sentence. The same qualities that made Radiguet a perspicacious observer of human nature gave him also some of the traits of an exploitative or manipulative friend or associate, continuing to measure and calculate even in the presence of those who felt closest to him.

Before long, having left Saint-Maur, Radiguet began to turn his critical gaze not upon his family, but upon his new Parisian friends—Misia Sert, Lucien Daudet, Constantin Brancusi, Jean and Valentine Hugo, and Jean Cocteau—as they gathered with him. Radiguet came to add a monocle and, on occasion, a cigar, to his "props," but the sphinxlike mien remained the same. Paul Morand's description of the unsmiling Radiguet is typical of many: ". . . with his myopic eye behind a huge monocle, smoking, with his somber, inscrutable countenance, a twelve-inch cigar . . . a wooden-faced Radiguet would watch us speak nonsense and act the fool, lending approval by his presence, yet reproachful in his taciturn, unrelenting arrogance, like the child judge of his parents."[24]

Paris after the War

Radiguet's entry into the artistic world of Paris took place in 1918, with the help of the writer André Salmon. Salmon, a friend of Picasso and of Apollinaire and a chronicler of artistic life in

Montmartre, was kindly disposed toward Radiguet's father, Maurice. Salmon was an editor at the daily newspaper *L'Intransigeant* and, knowing how hard it was for his friend to make ends meet and raise a large family on a cartoonist's earnings, agreed to accept two drawings a week from Maurice Radiguet for his front page. It was Raymond's assignment to deliver these. Before long, Salmon, out of loyalty to his friend, agreed also to accept the son's drawings, which were signed Raimon Rajky. Shortly thereafter, Salmon showed some interest in Raymond's writing and offered him some encouragement.

After four years of war, the stability of the *Belle Epoque* was little more than a fast-receding memory in Paris. Certainly, out of a fear of Bolshevism—the Russion Revolution had taken place in 1917, and the French army and navy continued their struggle against the Bolsheviks—a coalition of the right called the *Bloc National* swept to a landslide victory in 1919. To be sure, Charles Maurras, the reactionary leader of the right-wing monarchist movement *Action Française* was held to be the most influential thinker of his day by young writers, and his associate Léon Daudet, editor of the nationalist newspaper *Action Française,* was elected to the "Sky-blue Chamber"—so called for the color of the French army greatcoats. But, in this same, immediate postwar period, dada—international, anarchical, and irreverent—was becoming a force too vociferous to be ignored; all the more so with the arrival of Tristan Tzara in Paris from Zurich. And at the time of the *Bloc National,* André Breton and Phillipe Soupault were probing the unconscious, preparing the first major surrealist work, *Magnetic Fields,* an experiment in automatic writing performed while in a trance. On the surface, Catholicism, nationalism, and tradition may have seemed more firmly entrenched than in a very long time. In 1920, for example, Joan of Arc's canonization by Pope Benedict XV was officially sanctioned by an administration that was overwhelmingly nationalistic and predominantly Catholic; in the same period, for the first time under the Third Republic, envoys were exchanged between Paris and the Vatican. But the wind of revolt was also blowing strong. World War I, in the words of one contemporary chronicler, "is already something other than a war; it is a revolution."[25] Values were being adopted and discarded and constantly questioned. Apprehension or anxiety was so widespread a mood as to have become a cliché. Upon being introduced to Maurice Martin du Gard, Henry de Montherlant stated first his quest for meaning: "Four cults keep me busy at present—the human body, the sporting hero, the dead, the unknown soldier. What we need is to restore the divine to the earth." But then he added quizzically: "I hope that you are not anxious. That you do not get caught in that trap."[26]

The morality of this postwar period was as unruly or diverse as the rest of life. Observing the scene with complete cynicism—they had the impression of having seen every type of deviation—were the newspapermen. Many of André Salmon's journalist colleagues met at the café du Croissant in Montmartre, where by coincidence the great Socialist leader Jean Jaurès had been shot. When Radiguet suggested doing some newspaper pieces, in order to earn some money, Salmon weighed the ugliness of Parc Saint-Maur against the libertinage of the journalists and decided to help the youth place his newspaper articles: ". . . I still wished to help the family in Parc Saint-Maur, and the little poet interested me. I could have painted for him a picture of the dangers of newspaper work, but I already knew that it is utterly pointless to say such things to someone whose mind is made up. And then, Parc Saint-Maur! . . ."[27]

André Salmon

Salmon's account of his meetings with Raymond Radiguet is valuable not just because it shows that he, like others, was impressed by the youth's precocity, but because it gives us a glimpse of the genteel—but unpleasant—penury that attended Radiguet's life at that time. Salmon has no hesitation in calling Parc Saint-Maur "hideous"; and his house is labeled a "middle-class Bastille."[28] Moreover Salmon could not help noticing the poorly dressed appearance of the boy, who had turned up in his office in long pants obviously shortened from a pair belonging to his father. It is no doubt against this background of relative poverty that Radiguet determined to banish material concerns from his work: as a result, perhaps, of having been their prey as a child. His rejection of realism—specific information about the way his characters look, dress, or earn their living, what they eat, what they earn—may be an aesthetic choice; but this choice may well have been colored by his embarrassment at his own straitened circumstances as a child, and the wish to forget them.

It is difficult to understand just what it was in Radiguet's appearance that caused his associates invariably to remember their first meeting with him, or to explain the respect and even awe he inspired in seasoned habitués of life in Paris. The image that has been transmitted is of a boy short in stature, with unruly hair, and who was extremely nearsighted; he came to wear a monocle to correct this. Salmon perceived an expression of latent cruelty about Radiguet's face. His reserve and taciturnity were part of an aloofness that impressed most observers. All were struck by his maturity, and one commentator attributed this to the difficulties Radiguet must have known as a child:

This gaunt adolescent, too small, too nearsighted, seemed as it were embarrassed by his lack of resources, for he displayed great caution in all of his gestures and only advanced with great care. Yet one could detect in him an intangible element of virility and strength, behind that frail appearance. His speech, both precise and unhurried, showed willpower rare at his age: his words revealed a degree of discrimination, an evenness of temper, wit, and judgment that one does not usually find among people who have not suffered in their youth. Raymond Radiguet bore the stigma and the aura of all children whose life first began with hardship, suffering, or poverty. His strength of character raised him above complaining or even referring to this, but, beneath his studied sweetness, his grace and friendliness, one could perceive the edge of horror that had surrounded the first years of his life.[29]

With Salmon's help, Radiguet was soon able to find work doing newspaper assignments for *L'Eveil, L'Heure, Le Rire,* and *Fantasio.* Even before this, in May 1918, his first creative work, a short prose piece called "Galanterie Française" (French gallantry) appeared in *Le Canard Enchaîné,* signed Raimon Rajky. Other pieces—critical articles and poems—followed, appearing in *Sic,* one of the most inventive journals of the avant-garde, and in Breton's journal *Littérature,* which was to become the organ of surrealism. Radiguet began corresponding with a number of leading artistic figures, including Tristan Tzara, one of the principal founders of dada, who accepted a poem for his *Anthologie Dada.*

Within a few months of his debut in Paris, Radiguet seemed poised for a career in the iconoclastic vanguard of French literature at one of the very most exciting moments in the capital's artistic history. Salmon considered Radiguet to be too avant-garde, too fond of the typographical experiments characteristic of the period and practiced by Apollinaire and P.-A. Birot (the director of *Sic*) among others. Apollinaire himself, whose experimental collection *Calligrammes* came out in 1918, was made indignant that year by receiving from Radiguet some of the latter's poems, which he took to be a pastiche of his own work![30]

In complete contrast to slow suburban life, life in Paris was led at a hectic pace. Throughout the war years, one artistic wave after another had broken upon the capital, and a large, active avant-garde had formed, eager to plunge into new movements, exclaiming, in the words of one writer: ". . . we are CUBISTS, FUTURISTS, SIMULTANISTS, UNAMINISTS, . . . ISTS, . . . ISTS, in a word, NOWISTS."[31] Scattered among the experimental writings ("Air-plane . . . poem to be shouted and danced") and the manifestos ("the French tradition IS TO DENY TRADITION Let's follow the tradition")[32] was a widely held conviction that the new art would come to full fruition when hostilities came to an end. What is more, to a large extent the promise was kept. Radiguet found himself, once he had embarked upon life in Paris, exposed to talents as real and yet as diverse as those of Stravinsky, Satie, and the Six;[33] Brancusi and Gris and Pablo Picasso; Guillaume Apollinaire, Breton, Aragon, Reverdy, and Valéry; as well as Max Jacob and Jean Cocteau, who assumed enormous importance in his life, and many others.

Radiguet and Jacob

From the moment he came into contact with Salmon, Radiguet found the pace of his life quickening. The movement was vortical, as he moved with giddy speed into the center of Parisian artistic life. Salmon in turn presented Radiguet to Max Jacob, an extraordinary Breton poet of Jewish extraction who converted to Catholicism in 1909, after seeing Jesus in his room: "It is on my wall, at no. 7, rue de Ravignan, that he appeared to me September 28, 1909, at 5 o'clock . . . 5 o'clock in the afternoon."[34] We shall never know the full extent of the part played by Jacob in Radiguet's life. He obviously had an immense influence on the young man's artistic development. He immediately recognized Radiguet's talent as a poet, commenting in a letter: "You have a natural gift for making things stand out, for directness in your pieces. You are able to evoke things powerfully, with a single word, like our best friends. I do not know if you are our future national poet, but you deserve it as much as Y or Z."[35] It has not been realized to what extent Jacob shaped the form that much of Radiguet's work would take. In addition, Jacob introduced him to the painters Modigliani, Juan Gris, and Picasso and the writers Reverdy and Breton, to whom Radiguet would remain very close until his association with Cocteau drew him away. Perhaps just as important as all of the above is the possibility—and it is no more than this—that Jacob initiated Radiguet in homosexuality.

In 1919, when they met, Jacob was already the published author of *Le Cornet à dés* (The dice-box), one of the most important collections of prose poems ever to appear in France. Earlier, his conversion to Catholicism had caused a stir in Montmartre, where he had worked with Picasso at the *Bateau Lavoir* (Laundry boat). But it was neither as author nor convert, perhaps, that Jacob, at that time was best known. Pulling him in the direction diametrically opposed to that of the Cross—and causing him periods of great remorse and anguish—was the call of the flesh. Max Jacob was a homosexual, at least as well known for his pederasty as for his other qualities or idiosyncracies. We shall probably never know for sure exactly what happened between Jacob and Radiguet. They may indeed have begun a homosexual friendship, either because Jacob seduced the younger writer or because Radiguet, out of opportunism or for whatever motive, may have seen fit to encourage the affair.

Radiguet, though only sixteen, was far from being a naive stripling; when he was barely fifteen, he had carried on an affair with the wife of a soldier from his hometown: this affair became the heart of his novel *Devil in the Flesh*.

Apparently Radiguet first met Alice, the model for Marthe in *Devil in the Flesh*, in April 1917 while taking the train home from Paris; she was in the company of his father. At that time she was engaged to one Gaston, whom she married shortly thereafter while he was on leave. Alice's home was in Champigny, not far from where Radiguet's family lived. The two conducted a scandalously obvious affair, which was the talk of their respective towns. By the time he was fifteen, Radiguet was very much the one in charge, treating his partner rather callously, and this in spite of the fact that she was some ten years his senior! André Salmon has underlined the domination by Radiguet of those around him, including even the hardened journalists who congregated in the café du Croissant: "Perhaps he frightened them a little. I shall not venture to say they were really fond of him. No, he was simply king, this kid from Parc Saint-Maur, who had not felt the need to climb to the top of Père-Lachaise, where he was to go and sleep so quickly, in order to take the measure of Paris."[36]

Radiguet's domination of Marthe and of others must be attributed to his extraordinary will and character; certainly it was surprising, in view of Marthe's age, size, and handsome appearance: "The little fellow was small enough for Marthe to have been his mother, while remaining lovely Marthe. She was the boy's mistress. . . . A real beauty. . . . Marthe would cry as little as possible; but cry she did. The boy made her suffer in various ways. Marthe would disclose her grief to these gentlemen of the press." And Salmon repeated, by way of emphasis, the curious power Radiguet exercised over those around him: "I really think that the boy inspired fear. Marthe was pitied by these men, but less, or no more than, the boy was admired. Did they hate him? He made them uneasy, held sway over them."[37]

Unlike the Marthe of *Devil in the Flesh,* Alice did not die in childbirth. But it seems certain that the publication of the novel caused husband and wife much grief. There is some question whether their child might in fact have been fathered by Radiguet. Some thirty-five years later, a few years after Alice's death, Gaston was still trying to explain away the rumors by alleging that Radiguet had stolen his wife's private diary.[38]

It is possible that the friendship between Max Jacob and Raymond Radiguet may have remained on a Platonic rather than a Socratic plane. In any case, shortly after meeting Jacob, and probably thanks to him, Radiguet was introduced to Jean Cocteau. The two men lived out a homosexual friendship that is quite without precedent if appraised in terms of the artistic and aesthetic intensity that each achieved through contact with the other. Expressed more simply, Cocteau wrote some of his best work while under Radiguet's influence and defined himself adequately as an artist for the first time; and Radiguet's major writings were to be completed thanks to the guidance of Cocteau.

Cocteau and Radiguet

By 1919 Jean Cocteau's brilliance was universally recognized. Most recently he had presented the "realist ballet" *Parade,* with the joint participation of Diaghilev and the *ballets russes,* Erik Satie, and

Picasso, while his first major text of criticism, *Le Coq et l'Arlequin* (The Rooster and the harlequin), dedicated to Georges Auric and passionately committed to the "new music" of Erik Satie, confirmed Cocteau's position as the most versatile and visible standard-bearer of the Parisian avant-garde. In 1919, with his newspaper articles entitled *Carte Blanche,* Cocteau now continued his defense of the younger composers, praising the Six, whose unofficial impresario he became, but also lauding the poets and painters whose acquaintance he had made in Montmartre and Montparnasse from 1915 on: André Derain and Picasso, Max Jacob and Apollinaire. Cocteau's commitment to the here and now and his rejection of the past seem, in retrospect, extreme. He went so far as to denounce not just Mussorgsky and Wagner, but even Saint-Saëns and Debussy, and any composer indulging in symbolism or liquid sonorities: "Enough of clouds, waves, aquariums, water-nymphs and fragrances wafted at night; we need a music on *terra firma,* an everyday music."[39] Although Cocteau called for native, French music, he was willing to admit the American jazz band as a legitimate, healthy influence, alongside the circus and the music hall. To these accomplishments, one might add Cocteau's antirealist novel *Le Potomak,* which, dating from 1913 and dedicated to Stravinsky, may have been inspired by experiments in automatic writing, and his successful experimental poem *Le Cap de Bonne-Espérance* (The Cape of Good Hope), dedicated to the airman Roland Garros, which was published in 1919.

If, in 1919, Cocteau's brilliance was unquestioned, his profundity most certainly was. At about the time Cocteau was drawing close to Radiguet, André Gide published an open letter to him, in which he reminded him that he was little more than a nimble entertainer, a squirrel of the arts, hopping from branch to branch, and lacking in rigor or concentration.[40] Notwithstanding the personal rancor that often tended to fuel Gide's animosity toward Cocteau, there is some truth to his judgment. In 1919, Cocteau turned thirty. He had made his debut some eleven years earlier. For someone who had remained as constantly in the news as he had, his literary achievements were actually quite slim. To be sure, this is not to detract from some of his real accomplishments in promoting new art forms. Most seriously, however, it was impossible, looking back over Cocteau's eleven-year career, to detect any real direction or tenaciously held center to his work. His earliest manner, as expressed in the poetry collection *Le Prince Frivole* (The frivolous prince), was filled with anemic, pseudosymbolist conceits.[41]

In the early years of the war, Cocteau changed his style completely, churning out a long—twenty-seven four-line stanzas—"Hymne" addressed to General Joffre, the supreme commander of the French armies and victor of the first battle of the Marne, celebrating the future victory over the "Muse of Heinrich Heine and the Nine Symphonies."[42]

Another year, 1916, another change occurred, as Cocteau began to espouse the cause of the militant avant-garde. His startling transformations were just one element among several that caused some of the leaders of the new art movements to distrust him. Apollinaire, toward the end of his life (he died in 1918), distrusted Cocteau enormously. André Breton, closely associated with dada in 1919, wrote to Tristan Tzara, its leader: "My completely disinterested feeling, I swear to you, is that he (Cocteau) is the most detestable creature of this period."[43]

As early as 1908, Marcel Proust had taxed Cocteau with his lack of seriousness. Detecting in the younger man a writer of talent, Proust expressed his regret that he should spend so much time in society, dissipating his talents, instead of concentrating seriously upon his work.[44]

Without question, Cocteau lacked seriousness, whereas Proust did not, and Gide and Breton possessed it in overabundant supply. But Radiguet too was serious in his demeanor, his mental makeup, his readings, and his literary judgments. To a considerable degree he was the "some event" that Proust had hoped would wreak a change in Cocteau's attitude toward his craft.

Increasingly, as he became the protégé of Cocteau, Radiguet would spend the night in Paris, staying in small hotels in the rue Lavoisier or the rue de Surène, close to the Madeleine church, in the vicinity of the rue d'Anjou, Cocteau's home address. Even earlier, at the time of his closest contact with Max Jacob, Radiguet had shown a frequent inclination to miss the last train home, and stay on in the city with Reverdy, or Juan Gris, who became his friend, or Maurice Raynal. His room appears to have been in a state of unusual untidiness, strewn with volumes by Ronsard and Chénier, Malherbe and La Fontaine.

Before long, Cocteau and Radiguet struck their contemporaries as being inseparable. Radiguet's old clothes were replaced by more elegant items, designed by the couturier Jacques Doucet, whose interest in literature led him to pay retainers to a number of writers, including André Breton and Radiguet himself, in exchange for manuscript articles and letters. These pieces now form the nucleus of the Jacques Doucet Library, across the street from the Pantheon, in Paris. If Radiguet's clothes were now new, he still struck witnesses as being truculent: "Jean Cocteau . . . was followed by Georges Auric and by a small, young man, a false child, with a stick, a pink bow-tie, handsome teeth, heavy eye-brows, in a hostile silence, with his thick hair standing straight up from his stubborn brow."[45]

The writers' first collaborative effort was very much a Parisian item, a pure product of the times. It was called *Le Coq:* the cock or the rooster, playing on the first part of Coc-teau's name, on the traditional identity of the rooster as the bird of France, and on the perceived need to wake people up. At a time of intellectual ferment, the birth of new slogans, and superb, ephemeral journals to convey them, this broadsheet stands out as particularly brilliant and lively. The brief contributions by Cocteau, Radiguet, Poulenc, Durey, Auric, and others are presented in varied typographical formations, and the initial impression is that *Le Coq* is an unequivocal commitment to the avant-garde. Cocteau's deft, linguistic sleight of hand, with regard to dada, does not entirely dispel this impression; his position appears, to say the least, ambiguous. He refuses to be held to any one position, wishing to be both for and against left and right at the same time. He finds both left and right too timid, claims to have invented the extreme right, and to be close to an extreme left.[46]

One might well protest, as Radiguet did, that Cocteau's statements make little sense, except as clever-sounding phrases. If they could be interpreted at all, they would place Cocteau very close indeed to Mussolini and fascism; Mussolini founded the Fascist party in 1919 and would march on Rome in 1922. This may well have been a temptation for Radiguet, but for Cocteau . . . ? Hardly. Nonetheless, in spite of *Le Coq*'s novel typographic arrangements, and Cocteau's coy inability to dissociate himself fully and unequivocally from dada, the journal does represent an important date and turning-point in the two artists' aesthetic stance, with the beginning of a move toward more conventional, traditional, French forms.

There is about *Le Coq,* and indeed many of Cocteau's activities at this time, a sense of fun, and great artistic ease. The broadsheet itself was founded through a suggestion made at a dinner attended by Cocteau and his "clan" on March 6, 1920. These Saturday-night dinners were an excuse for Cocteau, Radiguet, and friends such as Valentine Hugo, Marie Laurencin, Lucien Daudet, Milhaud, Poulenc, Irène Lagut, and others to gather and enjoy themselves. Paul Morand described the group as a mutal admiration society, and it is thus that they are described in the first issue of *Le Coq*. After cocktails in an apartment—for example, that of Darius Milhaud in Montmartre—the friends would move on to a nearby restaurant for dinner, and often go to the Montmartre Fair, between the place Blanche and the place Pigalle: "After dinner, lured by the steam-driven merry-go-rounds, the mysterious booths . . . the din of the mechanical organs . . . we would visit the Fair of Montmartre, or occasionally the Cirque Medrano to see the Fratellinis in their sketches, so steeped in poetry and imagination that they were worthy of the *commedia dell' arte*."[47] These sights and sounds, experienced together in an atmosphere of conviviality, were a source of inspiration for musician and writer alike, according to Darius Milhaud.[48] Radiguet, notwithstanding his seriousness, a contrast to the high spirits of his companions, was readily accepted by the mutual admiration society.

It is a sense of playfulness that permeates Radiguet's joint ventures with Cocteau from this period. One such piece is the sketch *Le Gendarme Incompris* (The misunderstood gendarme). Written in the spring of 1920, it was first presented at the Theatre Michel in May 1921 as a "critique-bouffe" ("comic criticism") by Cocteau and Radiguet. This inspired piece of nonsense presents a gendarme who reports on shocking behavior by a priest (in fact a chatelaine in drag) to his superior, and quotes at length from Stéphane Mallarmé's prose work *Les Divagations*. Mallarmé's prose went unrecognized at first and *Le Gendarme Incompris* was assailed by the critics as being inane. On the same program as *Le Gendarme Incompris* were works by Max Jacob, Erik Satie, and also a play, by Radiguet alone, called *Les Pélican* (The Pelican family). This brilliant, absurd two-act play also dates from the spring of 1920. It is Radiguet's only complete, individual play. Its madcap humor and rapid action owe much to the film melodramas of the period, while the love interest (Mme Pelican, for example, loves her swimming instructor, and her daughter Hortense her photography teacher) is a mocking echo of the conventional boulevard drama. The play has about it a degree of freshness and an inventiveness that allow it to stand comparison with Ionesco's best creations. The daughter, for example, wishes to throw herself in the Seine; but it is frozen, and instead she wins a skating contest! The son, Anselme, wishes to be a jockey, while his father intends him to be a poet. But M. Pelican finally accedes to Anselme's wishes in a happy ending, which is for him a compromise: "Upon seeing you on horseback, I shall just have to imagine that you are riding Pegasus."[49]

Recurring throughout the four issues of Le Coq[50] that appeared in 1920 (it ceased to appear after that year) is the expressed desire to return to a more traditional, French form of art. The authors plead, in extremely modern, dadaist aphorisms, using novel typography, for a rejection of the modern: a curious oxymoron! The message is repeated in various guises: "Good Morning, Paris . . . Good-bye New York!"; "Latest News. Foundation of the Anti-Modern League. Return to poetry. Disappearance of the skyscraper. Reappearance of the rose"; "Bon voyage Oscar Wilde the paradoxical, Richard Wagner the sublime, . . . Alfred Jarry the mystifier."[51] Radiguet himself spoke out on behalf of Ronsard and in opposition to Rimbaud, praised the precious writing of the seventeenth century, and made a plea for banality or accessibility in writing.

In 1920, moreover, however much Cocteau might seem to be a leader of the avant-garde, it had become very difficult for him to be one in fact. The avant-garde was dada and its associates, most notably Breton. While Breton was eager to see Radiguet's name signed to articles in Littérature, he maneuvered diligently to keep Cocteau's out, in spite of Cocteau's many behind-the-scenes appeals. So, partly in response to Radiguet's natural interest in traditional French writing, partly because a position at the side of the avant-garde writers was being made impossible for him, and partly out of a desire to try something "new," Cocteau returned to the old, symbolized for him by the rose. There is irony in this development. Apparently under Radiguet's tutelage, Cocteau rediscovered the rose, the symbol of Ronsard, love, and the Renaissance. In point of fact, in his very first collections of poetry, La Lampe d'Aladin (Aladdin's lamp) of 1909, and especially Le Prince Frivole (The frivolous prince) of 1910, which he chose later to disavow, Cocteau had made considerable use of the rose as the quintessential image of life and beauty.

It also seems obvious that Radiguet, in nudging Cocteau back toward more traditional writing, was satisfying a personal urge as much political as it was aesthetic. Breton and his group represented a political left at the same time that they were the artistic avant-garde. Radiguet for his part made no bones about his preference for the right over the left, and in fact reproached Cocteau with timidity; Cocteau had asserted in *Le Coq* that *his* right-wing position was not political.

It seems perfectly clear that Radiguet's natural propensities were indeed conservative. It seems equally clear that it did not take much of an effort to guide Cocteau toward more traditional literary efforts. The change was not immediately evident. Cocteau wrote and presented his plays *Le Boeuf sur le toit* (The ox on the roof) of 1920, and *Les Mariés de La Tour Eiffel* (The wedding party on the Eiffel Tower) of 1921, both of which are avant-garde in character, like *Le Gendarme Incompris* and *Les Pélican.* However, at the same time that Cocteau was engaged in these productions, he collaborated with Radiguet on the "opéra comique" *Paul et Virginie,* based upon the novel by Bernardin de Saint-Pierre and set in Mauritius and Paris, which, by and large, was anything but avant-garde. The idea came from Radiguet, who had already written a poem called "Paul et Virginie" and, in addition, wrote the lyrics. The work is incomplete, since Radiguet did not supply all of the verse for which provision had been made in the text, and Satie did not provide the music, which had been anticipated in an announcement in *Le Coq.* This beautiful libretto, which was not published until 1967, is very reminiscent of the eighteenth-century sensibility of Bernardin, Marivaux, or Montesquieu, although the final (third) act is extraordinary in presenting Paul and Virginie's reunion, on stage, beyond death.[52] As in *Orphée,* the transition from life to death is presented as natural and indeed imperceptible. At the same time that Cocteau and Radiguet worked on *Paul et Virginie,* the older writer helped his companion to prepare for publication of the latter's volumes of poetry *Les Joues en feu* and *Devoirs de vacances.* Although these slim volumes would scarcely be called "classical," they are nonetheless in a more traditional, conventional manner than the first pieces he published.

In the summer of 1921, Cocteau fled the capital, as was his wont. Much of what he wrote was completed in relative isolation, in periods of intense concentration, during a summer vacation. This time, closer than ever to Radiguet, and somewhat possessive, he took

Radiguet with him. They went briefly to Auvergne, where they were displeased by the sullenness of the people they met, then moved on to the small hamlet called Le Piqueÿ, on the bay of Biscay, which faces the Atlantic. Far from Paris, the two enjoyed a period of creativity that is truly extraordinary, and the result of reciprocal influence and inspiration. This was the first of three summers spent together, each of which would result in a flurry of significant work by Cocteau and Radiguet alike.

In the company of Radiguet, and under his influence, Cocteau wrote, in the summer of 1921, his essay *Le Secret Professionnel* (Professional secret). It is the most important critical essay he ever wrote. In it he sets forth a program for himself as artist, asserting that the writer must divorce himself from avant-garde and public alike, and sound his own depths. Some of the ideas presented here owe little or nothing to Radiguet. For example, in places Cocteau is much closer to the surrealists, with whom he was on the worst possible terms, than he would openly admit. Like them he seeks a totality of vision in which antithetical modalities of reality: life and death, the real and the imaginary, the banal and the extraordinary, are not separated, but juxtaposed and seen as complementary. Like them, too, Cocteau stresses the irrational, seeing in the subconscious a source of knowledge to be invoked. And Cocteau here considers poetry—as Breton considered surrealism—a dangerous condition that may overpower its subject and make him addicted to it like a drug.[53] On the other hand, many of the notions expressed here do owe much to Radiguet. Cocteau's fascination with the angel as inspiration—youthful, vigorous, cruel, and a harsh voice of the conscience—derives from his fascination with Radiguet. Cocteau's repeated insistence upon clarity, classicism, and simplicity in writing echoes Radiguet's own words.

Cocteau by no means lived up to this program; but the best of his work follows it and, for the first time, it gave a very specific direction and center to his work. Radiguet, for his part, completed most of the novel *Devil in the Flesh*. Cocteau, in a benevolently despotic manner, would lock Radiguet up, and force him to write. Cocteau affirmed that, on vacation, Radiguet would shift from his Parisian regimen of frightful disorder to a more regular life; the change included a switch from alcohol to milk and water, and it is to this change that we owe much of his production. Back in Paris in the fall of 1921, Cocteau set about finding a publisher. Eventually, in 1922, when the final chapters of *Devil in the Flesh* had at last been completed, Cocteau withdrew the manuscript from La Sirène Editions and placed it with Bernard Grasset. The move was particularly astute. Grasset had earlier carried off a major coup, publishing Proust's *A la Recherche du temps perdu (Remembrance of Things Past)* when Gallimard had turned it down. More recently, Grasset had brought out the very successful Canadian novel *Maria Chapdelaine* and was on the lookout for a new best-seller. His needs were more than satisfied by the publication, in 1923, of *Devil in the Flesh*.

The summer of 1922 proved to be even more intense and productive than that of the previous year. At the beginning of May Radiguet and Cocteau, exhausted by the excesses of the season in Paris, left for the the Mediterranean. They went first to Le Lavandou, then to the adjacent village of Pramousquier, almost equidistant from Toulon and Saint-Tropez; at that time, the area was relatively deserted, not yet having been discovered by tourists. Radiguet corrected the proofs of *Devil in the Flesh* and, drawing his inspiration from literature—the great seventeenth-century novel *La Princesse de Clèves*—as well as from life—his acquaintance with the Count Etienne de Beaumont—wrote the major part of *Count d'Orgel*. Cocteau kept the promise contained in his personal manifesto—*Le Secret Professionnel*. In this most extraordinary creative period of his—or indeed any—life, he wrote two novels, *Le Grand Ecart* and *Thomas l'imposteur;* a volume of love poetry, *Plain Chant,* which must be counted among his best; and an adaptation of *Antigone* by Sophocles, which still retains much of its freshness. In addition, while Radiguet slept, he drew a number of beautiful sketches of him, later to be published as an album, in which love and desire are both apparent.[54] Radiguet's two novels and Cocteau's two have much in common; each is, in its way, a sentimental education, and each has phrases that could have come straight from a work by the other. Cocteau's homosexuality emerges—although still in rather gray relief—while Radiguet's *Count d'Orgel* reveals considerable sexual ambivalence or hesitation. On the plane of personal relations, the summer of 1922 was also a good one. Relations between Cocteau and Radiguet had a tendency to fluctuate, especially toward the end; but that summer they were as close as they would ever be. Moreover, Cocteau, at his own initiative, mended bridges to Gide, who received the epistolary overtures warmly and replied in kind. A harmonious group formed around Cocteau and Radiguet in the Var (the department in which Pramousquier is located), as they were joined by Georges Auric, Jean and Valentine Hugo (friends of long acquaintance, he was the great-grandson of Victor Hugo, while his wife had known Cocteau since 1914), and Pierre de Lacretelle, the brother of the more famous novelist Jacques. The only cloud to darken their happiness appears to have been the stepped-up attacks by the *Littérature* group, including Jacques Baron, Roger Vitrac, Benjamin Péret, and even Francis Picabia, who had been their friend. By October *Littérature* was including Radiguet, lost irretrievably to Breton and his cause, along with Cocteau and Max Jacob as objects of scorn. Hence this definition in the October 1922 issue of the journal: "Jean Cocteau: an angel's turd. Raymond Radiguet: a shovel for picking up an angel's turd."[55]

Radiguet and Cocteau returned to Paris in November, to find the literary milieu in distress over the death of Marcel Proust. Both attended the funeral to Père Lachaise cemetery on November 21, although they took a break from the long funeral cortege by going for a snack to one of their favorite haunts, the *Boeuf sur le toit,* whose proprietor was called Louis Moysès.

Le Boeuf sur le toit

Moysès had first run a bar called the Gaya, in the rue Duphot, which had become the headquarters for Cocteau, Radiguet, and their "clan." By irony and accident, not design, it was located very close to the Certa, the more solemn headquarters for Breton, Aragon, Soupault, and their associates in dada, in the Passage de l'Opéra. Moysès asked for permission to call his new establishment in the rue Boissy d'Anglais *Le Boeuf sur le toit:* "The Ox on the Roof." Cocteau, who had written the "ballet-pantomime" of that name, and Milhaud, whose music accompanied it, were happy to grant it. If relative seclusion amid the dunes of the South of France represent one dimension to Radiguet's life, *Le Boeuf sur le toit* is the other, or at least an appropriate metonymy for it. The contrast could not be greater between this cabaret and a sand dune, or the banks of the Marne for that matter.

Cocteau wrote of Venice: "On the Piazza San Marco, caught in a trap by this theatrical setting, this elegant throng confesses its most hidden secrets, as happens at a masked ball. The most frank impudence mates ages and sexes. The most timid individuals finally hazard there the gesture or the costume they longed for shame-facedly in London or in Paris."[56] The same might be said of *Le Boeuf sur le toit*. It stands as a curious epitome of the frenzied energy—both constructive and destructive—unleashed at the end of the war and continuing on through the 1920s. The period was not much more perverse than another, perhaps. But the war had swept aside many social and sexual conventions, prejudices, and barriers, so that, in *Le Boeuf,* one might find, at one moment, a play of contrasts, a juxtaposition of disparate elements, or a melting pot, which would have been inconceivable before World War I, in Proust's rigidly stratified society. Indeed, Proust himself came to *Le Boeuf* just four months before his death. It was at *Le Boeuf* that Radiguet would drink, before moving on to other parties, or would end the evening drinking, after the other parties, while listening to jazz played by the resident pianist, Clément Doucet, whom, on occasion, Jean Cocteau would accompany on the drums. Over the bar hung a painting of an eye, *L'Oeil Cacodylate,*[57] by Picabia, which looked down upon a company that might include Gabrielle "Coco" Chanel, the Prince of Wales, Arthur Rubinstein, or the Princess Marie Murat, in addition to Cocteau, Radiguet, Auric, or other members of their group. It was almost certainly at *Le Boeuf* that Radiguet met the rather mysterious Madame de Warkowska, who introduced him to opium smoking and is said to have remarked: "Opium?" Why make so much fuss? They smoked at my first communion, in Shanghai."[58] Here opium came out of its den, homosexuality was released from the closet and was in vogue, and there was an enervated desire to "try something new." In the words of Radiguet, repeating those of Apollinaire, from whom he is said to have heard them: "You've got to *do* things."[59] In this instance, Radiguet's program, understated and elliptical, runs parallel to that of Rimbaud, expressed more ambitiously in his letter to Paul Demeny and elsewhere.

So much freedom—license might be a more appropriate term—could not fail to turn Radiguet's head, mature though he might be. The story of his relationship with Cocteau is a chronicle of fruitful collaboration, reciprocity, and books written. But it is also a history of intermittent discord, growing greater with the passage of time. In the case of Radiguet, this would sometimes take the form of flight, to escape a presence that could become overbearing. In February 1921, for example, Radiguet ran off to Carqueiranne,

on the Mediterranean, in order to be away from his companion.
Cocteau, just three weeks later, dropped his business in Paris and
joined him! A year later, in January 1922, Radiguet and the sculptor
Brancusi, a friend of his, in an extraordinary display of taste for
adventure and rebellion, took off for Marseilles and Corsica. They
had just spent an evening with Cocteau and the "clan" at the opening
of *Le Boeuf*. At two in the morning, after leaving the cabaret, they
made up their minds to go south. Just a few hours later, they left
by train, with Radiguet still in his dinner jacket and unencumbered
by any luggage!

Radiguet's impatience with his mentor, and his refusal to accept
Cocteau as the only sentimental influence in his life, are shown also
by the affairs he conducted, in the few years leading up to his death,
with several women. Whereas Cocteau was unambiguously homosexual, Radiguet was not. He was a figure of considerable fascination
for the women with whom he came into contact. Some fifty years
after she fell in love with him, Irène Lagut, an early friend of
Radiguet's in Paris and a painter in her own right, as well as a
designer of sets for Cocteau, remembered the younger man with
great clarity and considerable emotion.[60] In 1921 Radiguet was
involved in a dalliance with the Englishwoman Beatrice Hastings,
who was considerably older than he and had herself been the mistress
of Modigliani in Montparnasse. She was an incorrigible composer
of plaintive letters and poems. The final stanza of one of the latter,
presented as an epistle to Jean Cocteau, gives some idea of the
amatory confusion in which she, Radiguet, and Cocteau could be
enveloped:

> I send you this note. I do love you both.
> I wander in the desert. I think with terror
> Of our hearts: deaf, mute, blind, in love.
> I know each of us loves—and I weep for all three.[61]

By the end of the year, Beatrice had been replaced in his affections
by Marie Beerbohm, whose uncles were the caricaturist Max Beerbohm—the incomparable Max—and the well-known actor Herbert
Beerbohm Tree. Beatrice reacted with considerable energy, as was
her wont; but so intertwined were life and literature for her that
she appeared as concerned about the effect of the break-up on her
writing as upon her emotional well-being; she wrote to "dear Ray-

mond": "I understand that Marie Beerbohm should wish to parade you in front of me, she is the kind of girl whose 'sensitivity' needs to triumph in public over her rival. . . . I am all the more bothered by this business since I need, for my own novel, to write very tenderly about you just now."[62]

In the last year of his life—1923—Radiguet would replace Marie Beerbohm with still another young woman, Bronya Perlmutter. She and her sister were said to be the daughters of an Amsterdam rabbi, of Polish stock. At the very time that Cocteau and Radiguet were involved in a different and extremely febrile form of collaboration— in effect "selling" Radiguet to as wide a public as possible—this liaison, and others, with both men and women, caused Cocteau much distress. There are few redeeming features or uplifting moral lessons that one can salvage from this final year. Radiguet appears to have entertained some idea of marrying Bronya Perlmutter, and she moved in with him. But his motives were not entirely noble, since he alleged that he did not want "to become a forty-year-old man called Mme Jean Cocteau."[63] On the other hand, in fairness to his "fiancée," who later became Mme René Clair, it must be stated that she did tend Radiguet with devotion until the last.

The Last Year

Whereas the summers of 1921 and 1922, if not the other seasons, have an aura of harmony, of creative energy harnessed and channeled by Radiguet, with Cocteau's help, the year 1923 gives a different impression. Little by little, Radiguet had been pulled into the Parisian vortex. In this final year, we see a life spinning out of control, a rapid unraveling, energy being transformed into entropy, disorder, and ultimate silence.

The future, from the outside, had never seemed brighter than at the beginning of 1923. As anticipated, *Devil in the Flesh* was published in March (on the tenth). Bernard Grasset's ability to recognize talent was equaled only by his genius for advertising. It may be "normal" for Grasset's contemporary authors—Glucksmann, Lévy, and the "New Philosophers," for example—to be featured in all of the news media. But in 1923 it was unprecedented to see Grasset on the newsreels in the cinema signing his check for 100,000 francs to a twenty-year-old writer! *Devil in the Flesh* became the center of a controversy in which Radiguet was accused of insulting the veterans of the war. But this did not hurt the sales, which were—and continue to be—excellent.[64] Cocteau, ever the impresario, appeared to be reliving and relishing the "scandal" he had provoked with *Parade,* in 1917. He made use of every means possible to secure favorable articles and interviews, and went so far as to sing the praises of Radiguet in an address at the Collège de France on May 3, 1923:

Raymond Radiguet appeared. He was fifteen years old and claimed to be eighteen, which mixed up his biographers. He never cut his hair. He was nearsighted, almost blind, he almost never opened his mouth. . . . If I talk to you at length about Radiguet and his book, it is because he seems to me one of the best examples of that attitude I would rather outline for you than extinguish by defining. . . . this child prodigy astonishes us by his lack of monstrosity. Rimbaud may be explained up to a point by the nightmares and the enchantments of childhood. One wonders where this bespangled magician puts his hands. Radiguet works with his sleeves rolled up, in full daylight.[65]

Cocteau continued his campaign into the month of May, successfully winning enough votes to have a new literary prize, the New World Prize, offered by a Washington lady to foster Franco-American friendship, granted to *Devil in the Flesh* over Phillipe Soupault's novel *Le Bon Apôtre* (The good apostle). It appears not to have troubled Cocteau a whit that a novel describing an affair between a schoolboy and the wife of a French soldier fighting with the Allies could scarcely promote such friendship! Cocteau went about his business influencing the jury. His own vote, and those of Max Jacob, Jacques de Lacretelle, and Bernard Faÿ, were sufficient to outpoll the opposition, made up of Giraudoux, Paul Morand, and Valéry Larbaud.

In the eyes of some, Radiguet's talent was immediately evident. As early as 1919, Max Jacob wrote words of high praise: "You are able to evoke things powerfully with a single word, like our best friends."[66] Grasset's confidence was such that, having read *Devil in the Flesh,* he offered to take all of Radiguet's writing. He continued, notwithstanding his enormous experience with distinguished writers, to say of Radiguet that he was the only writer in whom he had detected signs of budding genius.[67] Not all of the critics shared this opinion, however. While some resented Grasset's "selling" of his author, others found the work itself slipshod or mediocre at best:

The analysis of this book appears to me very simple. Here it is:

The author:	unknown.
The title:	an expression of Voltaire's.
The tale:	a colorless, banal news item; loves of a youth and of a married wanton.
The style:	undistinguished.
The morals:	corrupting.
The genre:	autobiography or fiction as you will. Advice to the author: have the good taste not to wash or pretend to wash your dirty linen in public: we already swallow enough germs and breathe in enough bad odors.
Summary and conclusion:	harmful for the young; bad for grown-ups; very dangerous and very useless for everybody.[68]

In April Cocteau was happy to show off his successful young friend in England, where he had been invited. Such was Cocteau's pride in his young charge that he wanted to display him as much as possible, and show him the world, while insisting that he keep on working. There were misgivings among the pair's friends that Cocteau might be pushing his friend too hard.[69]

It was rather typical of fluctuating relations between the two that, while the journey to England went off well, with visits to London, Oxford, and Harrow, Radiguet was eager, upon their return to Paris, to put distance between him and Cocteau. He took up residence in the Hotel Foyot, opposite the Luxembourg Gardens and above a famous restaurant where politicians from the Senate gathered. There he was joined by Bronya Perlmutter, and appears to have lived in the midst of complete disorder, with his room in an incredible mess, running up large bills for food and drink. Cocteau claimed that by May, Radiguet was downing a bottle of gin and a bottle of whiskey each day; he may well have exaggerated, however.[70]

According to Cocteau, summer was the time when Radiguet shifted from alcohol to milk and water. But the summer of 1923 was somewhat different. To be sure, Radiguet continued to work on *Count d'Orgel* at Le Piqueÿ for which he departed with Cocteau in July. However, this was not the customary period of quiet seclusion; at least it was less so than usual. Cocteau, Radiguet, and

Georges Auric were joined by a number of others including a rich American homosexual, Russell Greeley, and his friend the Count François de Gouÿ, who arrived from Paris. They appear to have encouraged Radiguet to follow their own heavy drinking habits, and the others, including the Hugos, had to hide alcohol from him; he obtained it in secret, however.

In June 1923 Radiguet had turned twenty. He was eligible for military service. According to the new law of June 29 of the year before, compulsory service had been set at eighteen months. However, thanks to the pleading of Bernard Grasset on his behalf, Radiguet was able to obtain a deferment until the end of December, in order to finish work on his new novel. Upon his return to Paris in the fall, in early October, he worked intermittently on the proofs, which had been given him by the publisher. But the quickened pace of his activities, in combination with increasing sickness and some apprehension accompanying the latter, was not conducive to concentrated work.

There is a tendency, in retrospect, to ascribe an appearance of destiny or fatality to these last months of Radiguet's life. The Hugos, for example, have recounted receiving threatening, premonitory spirit messages concerning the young man's impending death. Spiritualist séances were one of the less-healthy fads that swept Paris at this time. The surrealists were fascinated by them. Robert Desnos was able to slip into a trance without effort, and on a few occasions the danger of death—murder or suicide—for one or more of the participants in the séance was real. One account of several containing a prophecy of Radiguet's death is given in this description of a Ouija-board session. The participants spoke to the "spirit":

Cocteau insists:
—Tell us your name.
—Beauharnais.
—Keep on going.
— . . .
—Your first name?
—Flee!
—Why? Because we bother you?
—Yes.
—Is it because Radiguet is at the table that you don't answer?
—Yes.
Radiguet leaves the table. Cocteau says:

—Keep on going.
—I want his youth.
—Why?
—No comment.[71]

Just as his contemporaries invariably remembered the first time they saw Radiguet, so too several tell of the strangeness of one sort or another attending the last time they saw him. Jean Hugo wrote in his journal: "As our train for Paris was leaving early the next morning, we said good-bye that evening. Radiguet went with us to our door. While he was going off in the narrow corridor with its red carpet, a ceiling-lamp, concealed by a cornice, and located just above his head, illuminated his features violently and transfigured his face, which I was never to see again."[72] Bernard Grasset reported that at his last meeting with his young author, Radiguet took off his scarf and gave it to him as a keepsake.[73] There is undoubtedly something uncanny about these last months of Radiguet's life. On the other hand, it needs to be mentioned that Radiguet was still making plans for a literary future, including a novel on the life of a poet whom he admired greatly: Charles d'Orléans, the precursor of Villon in the fifteenth century.

The End

The death of Proust has about it an allure of noble dedication to art and, at the same time, inevitability. That of Radiguet, on the other hand, could probably have been avoided and is in no wise uplifting or suggestive of order or harmony. The circumstances have been quite well documented. As early as September, both Radiguet and Valentine Hugo were complaining of stomach pains. At the beginning of October, back in Paris, Radiguet continued to complain of pains. Toward the end of November, a number of companions commented on his pallor. Valentine, for her part, also felt increasingly sick. She was operated upon in Montpellier for peritonitis and made a speedy recovery. Cocteau's personal physician, Capmas, who had been unsuccessful five years earlier in treating Apollinaire, misdiagnosed the sickness as pneumonia, and Radiguet was treated with a hot toddy! Only when the worried Cocteau convinced Gabrielle Chanel of the seriousness of his illness was a proper diagnosis—typhoid—made. He probably contracted typhoid at Le Piqueÿ, eating contaminated oysters. He was rushed to the hospital in the rue Piccini. But in his condition, weakened already by the abuses of the previous years, his heart and liver could not hold out. He died about five A.M. on December 12. His mother could not be present, having herself contracted a mild dose of typhoid from her son. He died alone, in terrible agony, and it is said that his face was terror-stricken, as though he had woken up in the dark and realized he was going to die and was by himself.

Even Radiguet's funeral provoked some controversy. A number of friends rallied round to cover the costs of the hospital, the burial, and the bills he had run up at the Hotel Foyot. Louis Moysès canceled those incurred at *Le Boeuf.* So these matters at least were settled. But it was felt by many that his white coffin—Radiguet was not twenty-one—was hardly suitable for someone who had led as debauched a life as he had.

Missing from Radiguet's bedside in the hospital—fear of typhoid, or heartbreak?—and missing from the funeral was Jean Cocteau. For once, Cocteau was not there to "arrange things." The funeral was arranged, instead, by Gabrielle Chanel, who took care of all the details: from the service in the church of St. Honoré d'Eylau to the interment in Père Lachaise. In fact, Cocteau was overcome with grief and only emerged from the initial shock into a kind of abulia: from despair to profound melancholy. It was from this period on that Cocteau would become addicted to opium.

Later, Cocteau would indeed attempt to "arrange things" by creating a myth according to which this life and death were preordained, mapped out according to a divine plan. The facts about Radiguet's last months are well known. They comprise rounds of parties, bills unpaid, increasing sickness, work left uncompleted, and a dreadful death. To be sure, he did attempt to make some order out of his papers; but this gesture may be logically explained by his expectation of joining the army. Cocteau's description of the final period, given long after his companion's death, paints a different, orderly, meaningful picture. Cocteau claimed that Radiguet gave up his vices, slept well, and set his life in order in the final four months of 1923. Cocteau implied that he and the boy's parents had been present at his death, a peaceful departure. He provides a touching description of Radiguet's prescience shortly before his demise, and of the deathbed scene itself:

Listen, he told me on the ninth day of December, listen to a terrible thing. In three days I shall be shot by the soldiers of God. As I fought back the tears, he made up contradictory information, he continued: Your information is not as accurate as mine. The order has gone out. I heard the order.

Later on, he also said: There is a moving color, and people hidden in this color.

I asked him if I should get rid of them. He answered: You can't, since you don't see the color.

Then, he sank back.

His mouth moved, he spoke our names, gazed in astonishment at his mother, his father, and his hands.[74]

Unfortunately, this picture, beautiful though it may be, is not at all true, and it is impossible for us to accept that Radiguet's death was as "neat," inevitable, orderly, or meaningful as Cocteau claimed.

Chapter Two
Poetry

Although Radiguet is much better known as a novelist than as a poet, the number of poems he wrote is substantial, and it is as a poet that he made his literary debut. In December 1919, the writing of prose was still a novelty for him, as he makes clear in a letter to the literary patron Jacques Doucet:

Dear Mr. Doucet:
I am sending you by the same mail a rather short chronicle, for at the moment I am working on a novel. I am truly happy to do these chronicles for you, for this gives me a taste for writing in prose which is, I think, very useful. So if, perchance, my novel were interesting, I would have you to thank, for you gave me the idea of writing in prose.[1]

Radiguet's poems date essentially from the years 1918 to 1921. The principal collection, *Les Joues en feu (Cheeks on Fire)* comprises some thirty-four poems and was published posthumously in 1925. It was preceded by two rather slim volumes: a first version of *Les Joues en feu* (1920), and *Devoirs de vacances* (Summer assignments) of 1921. Radiguet's production also includes the two-manuscript collection *Le Bonnet d'âne* (The dunce's cap) and *Couleurs sans danger* (Harmless colors), which are both dated 1919 but did not appear until after the author's death. Still another slim, posthumous book is called *Jeux Innocents* (Innocent games) and was published in 1926 for the first time.[2] A number of pieces were first presented in some of the literary journals of his time; some were gathered into Radiguet's collected volumes of poetry, but others were not. The publication of his *Oeuvres Complètes* (Complete works) brought to light, some thirty-six years after Radiguet's death, even more previously unknown poems. There is finally a small volume entitled *Vers Libres* (Free verse). These pornographic pieces had first been published in 1925. Cocteau, Grasset, and Radiguet's family had immediately asserted that most of these were not by Radiguet. In 1967 they were republished in Italy, in a volume entitled *Raymond Radiguet:*

Gli Inediti.[3] In spite of Cocteau's denial, it now seems clear that this licentious verse was indeed by Radiguet.

Radiguet and Rimbaud

It is regrettable that Radiguet's poetry is not better known. These small, crafted pieces have none of the philosophical ambition of, say, the French romantics. On the other hand, they bear comparison with the incidental but worthwhile verse of poets such as Tristan L'Hermite or Parny. Apart from their intrinsic merit, which is real, they are a remarkable document of one young writer's response to the shifting poetic currents of his time: one of the most exciting periods in modern French literature. Radiguet's ear was as attuned to the literary movements around him as any writer's, and this is shown in the development of his poetry from the first pieces, which appeared in avant-garde journals, to his manuscript collections and the subsequent small volumes.

The very brevity of Radiguet's career, his precocity, and his untimely death make inevitable a comparison with Rimbaud. Cocteau was not at all averse to linking the two names, comparing the "Rimbaud miracle and the Radiguet miracle,"[4] or presenting both together as prodigies.[5] Radiguet's association with Cocteau, his fondness for the Marne River, his participation in the Saturday-night dinners with his artist friends, his rather bohemian existence and the prevalence of childhood as a theme in his work recall similar patterns in Rimbaud's life and work: Rimbaud's association with Verlaine, his descriptions of the Meuse River, his attendance at the monthly banquet of the Parnassian poets *(les Vilains Bonshommes)*, and so on. In the welter of impressions and even coincidences that suggest a parallel between the two writers, it is perhaps easy to forget that the differences or divergences are great. Above all, the trajectory followed by Rimbaud is quite different from Radiguet's itinerary. Whereas Rimbaud moved away from fixed forms to free form, out of tradition toward experimentation, Radiguet came to abandon the avant-garde, and to espouse the cause of order, clarity, and structure. Rimbaud made no attempt to conceal or sublimate his loathing for his hometown, Charleville, its pettiness, the tyranny of custom that reigned there, and he represented his young protagonist as an outsider. "A la Musique" (The band) is just one of the many early pieces showing his contempt and hatred. As the towns-

people listen to a military band in the railroad square of Charleville,
the poet slinks about in the background, impatient, mentally un-
dressing the girls he sees:

> Sur la place taillée en mesquines pelouses,
> Square où tout est correct, les arbres et les fleurs,
> Tous les bourgeois poussifs qu'étranglent les chaleurs
> Portent, les jeudis soirs, leurs bêtises jalouses
>
> —L'orchestre militaire, au milieu du jardin,
> Balance ses schakos dans la *Valse des fifres:*
> —Autour, aux premiers rangs, parade le gandin;
> Le notaire pend à ses breloques à chiffres.
> ....
> —Moi, je suis, débraillé comme un étudiant
> Sous les marronniers verts les alertes fillettes:
> Elles le savent bien, et tournent en riant
> Vers moi, leurs yeux tout pleins de choses indiscrètes
> ....
> J'ai bientot déniché la bottine, le bas . . .
> —Je reconstruis les corps, brûlé de belles fièvres.
> Elles me trouvent drôle et se parlent tout bas . . .
> —Et je sens les baisers qui me viennent aux lèvres . . .

> (On the square cut up into measly lawns,
> A square where everything is just right, both trees and flowers,
> All the wheezing bourgeois, stifling in the heat,
> Bring their jealousies and stupidity on Thursday evenings.
>
> The military band, in the middle of the garden,
> Sways its shakos to the *Waltz of the Fifes:*
> The dandy struts around in the first rows,
> And the notary is suspended from the numbers on his watch-chain.
> ....
> —While I, unkempt as a student, follow every move,
> Under the green chestnut trees, of the lively girls:
> They know this, and laughingly turn
> Their gaze full of indiscretions upon me.
> ....
> In no time, I have located their boot, their stocking . . .
> —Ablaze with fine fevers, I piece together their bodies.
> They think me funny and talk in a whisper . . .
> —And I can feel kisses puckering my lips . . . [6]

From a first rejection of town and country, family and church, Rimbaud's work became a denial and refusal of all conventions, an affirmation of complete freedom:

I say one must be a *seer,* make oneself a *seer.* The Poet makes himself into a *seer* through a lengthy, huge, calculated *disordering of all his senses.* Every form of love, suffering, madness: he searches by himself, draining within himself every poison, and keeping only their quintessence. Unutterable torture for which he needs all of his faith, all his supernatural strength, and which makes him, of all men, the great ill one, the great criminal, the great accursed one,—and the supreme Sage!—For he attains the unknown! Since he has nurtured his soul, which was already rich, more than anyone![7]

Radiguet went in just the opposite direction. His early work bears the marks of poetic experimentation of the period, such as novel typographical arrangements, frequent punning, ellipses, and resulting obscurity. Eventually however he came to adopt regular verse forms and conventional subjects, whereas Rimbaud, a pioneer, had moved from standard forms to the freedom afforded by the prose poem. As a corollary of this first difference between the two poets, there is a second, very important one. Radiguet's ambition was in no wise as wide-ranging as that of Rimbaud. He was much too detached and ironic to undertake vast poetic enterprises such as making himself a seer. In this relative coldness, detachment, and skepticism, he was also quite different from Jean Cocteau. Unlike Cocteau or the surrealists, he set no store by dreams.[8] Religion, the supernatural, and spiritual elements have practically no place in his work. His narrow, concentrated—but very real—talents are comparable, in the first poems he wrote, to those of the cubist painters, to the extent that he treats simple subjects, viewing them from different points of view. Increasingly, he came to a willing acceptance of restraint, tradition, and structure, and his themes narrowed, becoming centered upon love, pleasure, desire. In this later phase, as he inscribed himself within a tradition, not outside it, many of his pieces are comparable to the finely crafted poems of the eighteenth-century rococo period, modest in scope, and preoccupied with the pleasure of this world. Throughout his brief career, Radiguet's poetry concentrates upon the physical, visible world, largely to the exclusion of philosophical or metaphysical questions; it is almost never an interrogation of the nature of being or of first causes.

Poetic Beginnings: Experimentation

It is some measure of Radiguet's precocity that his first published poem appeared in the same month—June 1918—that the poet himself turned fifteen. Signed "Raimon Rajky" and entitled simply "Poème," it came out in the avant-garde journal *Sic*. In the months that followed, Radiguet contributed a number of other poems to the same journal.

From its founding, in 1916, *Sic* had made itself the advocate of change, of innovation in the arts. In February 1916, a dithyrambic article sang the praises of futurism: ". . . your faith is beneficent; we must consider you valuable generators of intellectual activity, you love the unknown, you love life, your ambitions are limitless, for all these reasons we must love you."[9] *Sic* championed first futurism, then cubism, then welcomed dada. Its leading contributor was Guillaume Apollinaire. Others included Drieu la Rochelle, Reverdy, Cocteau, Soupault, Breton, Tzara, Jacob, and of course its editor, P.-A. Birot. Its subtitle—*Sons Idées Couleurs Formes*[10]—gives an accurate idea of its vitality, enthusiasm, and exuberance, and its eagerness to foster and bear witness to the new in all of the arts. With the death of Apollinaire in late 1918, most of the wind was taken out of its sails. The memorial issue of January-February 1919 was, to be sure, large and had contributions from many of the major artists of the period, including Aragon, Birot, André Billy, Cendrars, Cocteau, Max Jacob, Picabia, Reverdy, and Tzara. An article by Louise Faure-Favier appeared as the voice of Apollinaire, sounding from beyond the grave, undiminished:

> Do not weep, my friend Louise. Here I am, dead! But it is not tiresome at all to be dead. On the contrary it is very interesting. It is very curious. Already I am discovering the other side of things. Everything is brand new in Death, much more than in Life. It is a great unexplored field.[11]

In point of fact, in late 1919, its articles no longer seemed—or were—exciting, and it stopped appearing at the end of that year.

Radiguet's contributions to *Sic* were not out of place alongside the other bold, experimental forms. In a period when Juan Gris, Georges Braque, and Picasso were the friends of the poets, and were making use of newsprint collages, while Apollinaire lauded Picasso and allowed the theme of his "Calligrammes" to dictate the typographical shape of the poem on the page, Radiguet joined the cubist chorus. His "Poème" of June 1918 has much in common with his later work: a simple subject, the dispassionate treatment of a visual image, and an absence of lyricism. But what first strikes the reader is less the subject—a domestic garden scene—than the *visual* appeal of the words:

> un édredon rouge à la fenêtre
> des fleurs dans l'entrejambe du ca-
> leçon   ce jardin tiède dans la giroflée
> parfum de linge tiède séché
> le marronnier chante
> serait-ce ces bougies roses irrégulièrement
> plantées ou bien   un   oiseau
>
> su la co d le li g   d n e
>   r   r e   n e a s
>
>   e i   a ch   e q   m
>   ch m se m n ott   ui   e
>
>   t   d l s br
>   en   e   as
>
> (a red eiderdown at the window
> flowers between the legs of the under-
> pants   this warm garden in the wallflower
> a fragrance of warm, dried clothes
> the chestnut tree sings
> would it be these pink candles unevenly
> planted or else   a   bird
>
> o the l n the cl the d n e
>   n   i e   o   s a c
>
>   ne r e   i   wh
>   o   a m d sh rt   ich
>
>   re ch   o t t m
>   a es u o   e)[12]

In subsequent poems, Radiguet was more conservative in the typographical layout of the words: he may well have heeded the advice of André Salmon, who found such exercises gratuitous, or he may have been affected by Apollinaire's displeasure at seeing what appeared to be a pastiche of his own work. On the other hand, in keeping with the fashion of the time, first set by Apollinaire, none of Radiguet's poems to appear in *Sic* had any punctuation.

It took Radiguet very little time to acquire some of the images and techniques of cubism and the New Spirit, as is evident from another "Poème" published in the November issue of *Sic*.

Ligne d'horizon

Morceaux de tête

Dans le rocking-chair
            Murs
        L'éphéméride est déjà à après-demain
Un camion automobile écrase nos ombres
                                    S.V.P.
On se bouscule aux portes du ciel ou des Grands
magasins
                        Les paroles se cognent
Articles pour voyage mais
    Il y a plus de monde au rayon des ustensiles de
    cuisine l'é-
    Charpe des maires
            Au   bout des rails
                    La   mer
(OC, 1:112)

The subject or frame of reference is given in the first line: "Line of horizon." The image of a person moving to and fro in a rocking-chair leads the poet to break down this movement into its positions in space, like still photographs: "Pieces of head / In the rocking-chair." Like Apollinaire or Cendrars, Radiguet has recourse to images of vehicles, to express his impatience with the past and his eagerness to move into the future. His calendar is opened "at the day after tomorrow" as he entreats a truck to "crush our shadows / If You Please." The gaze shifts to a large department store, to its travel-goods section, then its kitchen appliances, and finally to the image of the far distant sea "At the   end of the rails."

The borrowings in "Line of horizon" are rather obvious; nonetheless it is an adroitly executed poem. Like many a cubist painting, it draws attention to itself as composition. The first major literary influence on Radiguet was Jacob, and it may well be that Jacob's fondness for punning "rubbed off" on Radiguet. Just as the cubist painters used geometric patterns of forms to establish a visual dynamic independent of the subject depicted, so Jacob explored the poetic possibilities of the pun to establish a dynamic of sound disrupting any notion of the poem as a unilinear representation of objective reality. Radiguet in turn follows a similar direction. There is, to be sure, some thematic unity in this poem: the starting point is what the poet sees on the "line of horizon"; in addition, there are the various "vehicles" from rocking-chair to truck, railroad to the boat implied in the final word "sea." But a subtler coherence is provided by sound repetition. After mentioning the travel-goods section in the department store, the poet adds that "There are more people in the kitchen-appliance section." Unspoken but implicit is the notion that this is the section to which mothers—*les mères*—would go. Immediately afterwards mention is made of the mayors—*les maires*—and the final reference is to the sea: *la mer*. Each of these words is of course pronounced in the same way, as [mɛ:r]. This punning effects a shift of focal plane that introduces an element of doubt and complexity that enriches the poem.

The prose poem "Tohu," which appeared in the December 1918 issue of *Sic,* gives a clear idea of how far Radiguet was at his beginnings from the canon of classical containment and order he later adopted. Tohu is a traveler who, having arrived on earth, makes his appearance in an automobile and sets up his "act" in a large square in the city. He wishes to display the sixth part of the world and perfection itself, upon claiming to have discovered them and to have registered the images on the retina of his eye. But the milling crowd, having perched in trees and arrived on the scene in streetcars, is not at all satisfied with the spectacle he puts on in his tent. While he screams, the crowd becomes a mob, then Tohu is declared an impostor by a scientist, knived, and shot! This grotesquerie is of course reminiscent of scenes from Jarry's *King Ubu* at a moment when Jarry was a favorite of the iconoclastic avant-garde. The very name Tohu, at the same time that it is part of the expression *tohu-bohu,* a Hebrew term suggesting primitive chaos, or a hubbub, reminds us also by its sound of the name Ubu. In places, the influence of Jacob's prose poems in *Le Cornet à Dés* also seems obvious.

1919—An Extraordinary Year

By 1919, recognition of Radiguet's talent as a poet was general
in avant-garde circles. In the February issue of *391*, which Francis
Picabia edited, Tristan Tzara wrote a "Chronicle" in homage to the
Parisian friends of dada and included Radiguet as one of the most
prominent among them. Max Jacob also recognized the young writer's talents and encouraged him in his art. Juan Gris linked Radiguet's name with that of Reverdy, whom Radiguet would later
repudiate in no uncertain terms; Gris wrote:

The most astonishing thing is the sudden crop of poets. Reverdy is one
of the leaders and one of the best; he has influenced a great many of the
younger ones. There are some extraordinary ones like Radiguet, who is
barely seventeen, and has written some charming things. It is the Reverdy
school that is most akin to our painting; they are breaking away more and
more from Cendrars and Tzara.[13]

In fact, it is a simplification to consider that Radiguet was "breaking
away" from Dada. With the decline of *Sic*'s importance, and its
eventual demise, a number of artists, including Radiguet, were
attracted to Dada. From January 1919 on, Radiguet, always an
opportunist, began a correspondence with Tzara, who was still in
Zurich. He sent him poems, with the hope that they would appear
in the fourth volume of the journal *Dada,* but then had second
thoughts about their worth and asked that they be withdrawn. But
the prose poem "A plusieurs voix" (With several voices) did appear
in May, in the *Anthologie Dada.* Subtitled "fragment de Tohu" it
is very much in keeping with dada's desire to jolt the reader and
cultivate paradox. The "several voices" are those of a group of unhappy people in a city square, reflecting upon their physical handicaps; the punctuation almost is suppressed, while alexandrines (lines
3 and 5) are interspersed with onomatopoeic letters; a blind man
comes into the square and tries to make sense out of the hubbub.
Eventually his sight is restored, but he is shocked by the ugliness
of his wife, and by how fierce the sunlight is:

Pardon monsieur
le monsieur c'est une dame
tous ces gens réunis sur la plus grande place

                                                          pleurent-ils
ah que je suis malheureux je n'ai qu'une bouche
                                        ne peux en baiser qu'une à la fois
je suis aveugle pourquoi n'ai-je pas deux yeux
                                                    comme mon père
j'ai deux yeux ils ne me servent qu'à pleurer
je n'ai que deux yeux si j'en avais quatre peut-
                                        être verrais-je mieux
être borgne je pleurerais deux fois moins
la lumière ne parcourt que trois cent mille
        kilomètres à la seconde quand elle arrivera
        dans ce pays je serai mort depuis longtemps
        hélas je ne verrai pas clair la lumière sera
        pour mes enfants
peut-être si je tue ma soeur j'aurais sa tranche
                                                          de soleil
   S S S   JA   RRIVE
ph ph brusque éclairage de phare puissant
ô ma femme si laide je la croyais belle elle s'est
                                        sauvée en me voyant
vite des canons
que la lumière fait mal aux yeux
au se
secours il vient nous assassiner avec cela qu'il
        veut nous faire croire être de la lumière
        que vient-il faire ici il faut le tuer, il n'est
        pas de notre pays; (*OC* I, 116–17)

(Excuse me sir
sir is a lady
all these people gathered in the main square
                                        are they weeping
oh how unhappy I am I have only one mouth
                                can kiss only one at a time
I am blind why do I not have two eyes
                                        like my father
I have two eyes they just let me weep
I have only two eyes if I had four perhaps
                                        I could see better
with one eye I would weep just half as much
light just covers three hundred thousand
        kilometers per second when it reaches
        this country I'll have been dead for a long time

        alas I won't see clear the light will be
        for my children
perhaps if I kill my sister I would have her share

                                                of sunlight
  S S S   IA   RRIVE
l l sudden illumination from powerful light
oh my wife so ugly I thought her lovely she has
                                run away upon seeing me
quickly guns
how the light hurts my eyes
he
help it comes and kills us withal it
        wants to make us think it is light
        what is it up to here must kill it, it is
        not from these parts;)

Radiguet was only one of several young writers, in 1919, to antic-
ipate eagerly the arrival of Tristan Tzara in Paris.[14] The pages of
Littérature, the new journal André Breton had just founded, wel-
comed·contributions by Tzara, and the star of the avant-garde was
very much in the ascendancy. Breton took malicious pleasure in
courting Radiguet also, and in publishing his pieces, while exclud-
ing Cocteau. In sum, 1919 was an extraordinary year for Radiguet
the poet, as a number of leaders of the avant-garde vied for his
commitment to their cause. It was a time of delicate equilibrium
for him in his friendships, insofar as he was close to Cocteau, Reverdy, Max Jacob, and André Breton. Such were the temperamental
and aesthetic differences among these artists that their confluence
could not last long; and it did not. But in 1919 Radiguet did not
yet have to choose for one, and therefore against the others. That
would come a little later.

   Two manuscript collections of poetry by Radiguet—*Le Bonnet
d'âne* (The dunce's cap) and *Couleurs sans danger* (Harmless colors)—
date from 1919. They were intended as a New Year's gift for his
sponsor, Jacques Doucet. The manuscript poems, accompanied by
watercolors of flowers executed by the poet, were not published in
Radiguet's lifetime. After his death, Jacques Doucet had them reproduced in a moving little volume entitled *In Memoriam,* which
also included a photograph of the poet by Man Ray, other manuscripts and letters, and the invitation card to Radiguet's funeral.

Of the ten poems in *Le Bonnet d'âne,* Radiguet considered only one, entitled "Incognito," worthy of inclusion in his major volume *Les Joues en feu.* Another piece, "Fac-similé," was reproduced in the 1920 *Joues en feu.* However, *Le Bonnet d'âne* is important for the light is sheds on Radiguet's development. In these poems, there are numerous passing references to the author, his developing poetic vocation, and his firm intention to make his mark as a writer. The title itself implies that he is aware that he is only starting out in his career and has not yet served his apprenticeship. However, in spite of the various outside influences on the pieces, it is clear that they reflect a deep sense of structure that is fundamentally opposed to dada's strivings.

The title "Incognito" in *Le Bonnet d'âne* is presumably a reference to the poet's still being unknown. In this poem, however, the author has no doubt about his future renown. The absence of punctuation and rhyme creates a—false—first impression of a lack of direction. In fact, the fourteen lines recall the order of the sonnet, to the extent, even, that the first eight could be considered as two quatrains:

> Soi-disant diseuse de bonne aventure
> On est presque nu
> Des portraits de famille
> Il y en a qui seraient honteux
> Une rue déserte
> Plus tard elle portera votre nom
> Les nuages descendent à terre
> Ils gênent nos pas
> Les hommes qu'on a mis en prison
> ne se doutent de rien
> Des bêtes féroces gardent la capitale
> Pourtant nous ne sommes pas bien méchants
> La clef des champs
> Je vous en prie (*OC,* 1:22)

The opening of the poem sets the mood of prediction of the future, then sweeps back immediately to the past, to an album of family photographs, the possible embarrassment at seeing oneself posed, naked:

A self-styled fortune-teller
One is almost naked
Family portraits
There are some who would be ashamed

Alone on the street, the poet states with conviction that it will be named after him; then, like a crystal ball fogging up, clouds roll down on the street:

A deserted street
Later it will bear your name
Clouds come down to the ground
They impede our footsteps

All is now obscured, so that even the men who have been put in prison are unaware of their predicament: "The men who have been put in prison / suspect nothing." The situation now seems intimidating or parlous, the capital not such an easy conquest, and the poet turns plaintive: "Ferocious beasts guard the capital / And yet we are by no means wicked." The reference to "ferocious beasts" may derive from Radiguet's crossing of the bois de Vincennes at night, on his way from Paris to St.-Maur; he always hoped that the animals in the zoo there would not roar out and frighten him!

In several other pieces, the poet appears preoccupied with himself and especially with his name. Cocteau had made good use of the pun in *his* name, *coq-tôt* ("early rooster"), exploiting the image of the rooster in the essays entitled *Le Coq et l'arlequin*.[15] Radiguet, having first signed his name Raimon Rajky, was now using his own name, but apparently with some reluctance; his friends bestowed upon him moreover a number of nicknames. In the poem "Il s'agit de moi" (It is about me) we read "Les lettres de mon prénom habituel s'envolent / Celui qui reste ne plaît à personne" ("The letters of my usual first name fly away / The one that is left pleases nobody") (*OC,* 1:132). This is presented in the context of a street vendor displaying a toy windmill for sale. The theme recurs in the poem "Au petit bonheur" (As chance dictates), set in the heart of winter: "This day was the shortest of the year / Various first names / Another much prettier."[16]

Ce jour fut le plus court de l'année.

Divers prénoms.
Un autre, bien plus joli.

It may well be that, in making frequent references to fording rivers, Radiguet was making a subtle reference to the last part of his own name, -guet, which has the same sound as the French word for a ford, *gué,* at the same time that he was remembering the Marne River: "Five minutes earlier / Everything was happening at the water's edge FERRYMAN / also / (When I am called)"

Cinq minutes plus tôt
Tout se passait au bord de l'eau   PASSEUR
aussi
(Quand on m'appelle)[17]

Almost all of these early poems involve rapid shifts, transitions from one plane of meaning to another. The link between these planes of meaning is now evident, now tenuous. The effect is to oblige the reader to focus attention on the very words on the page, rather than linger with the material reality that is first conjured up. The underlying aesthetic is very close to that propounded by Max Jacob in his preface to *Le Cornet à dés:* that a work of art has value in and of itself, rather than through the confrontation between it and the real world.[18] It is also, of course, close to that advocated by the cubists. And, finally, it is not unlike the "discipline" or the attention solicited by a movie; Radiguet was an avid moviegoer, as were most of his friends. One of the poems in *Le Bonnet d'âne* is in fact devoted to the cinema. Called "Tous droits compris" (All rights reserved), an allusion to the copyright notice on the film print—it presents its topic in the first line, as Radiguet's poems so often do: "Screen." Then, like the shifting images that a film may present, the images of the poem itself shift, from a detective in the movie trying to go unnoticed, to a brand name, probably advertised in the cinema, to memories of months past and flowers faded *outside* the theater, then back to the thief stalked by the detective, imitation flowers advertised on the screen, the close of the spectacle, and the final memory of these (movie-) stars who reappear nightly:

Ecran
Pour qu'on ne le remarque pas

Le détective fait semblant de sourire
                          Marque Azur
Où sont-ils?
Juin Mai   Mes roses véritables
                          Au voleur
        Garnitures   pour chapeaux
Les fleurs que voici
L'écran est blanc mais l'oeil se souvient
        Les étoiles de tous les soirs
                                    (OC, 1:135)

                          (Screen
So as not to be noticed
The detective pretends to smile
                          Azure brand
Where are they?
June May   My true roses
                          Stop thief
        Trimmings   for hats
The flowers we see here
The screen is blank but the eye remembers
        The stars of every evening)

Although the small collection entitled *Couleurs sans danger* (Harmless colors) dates, like *Le Bonnet d'âne,* from 1919, the poems in it are from the second half of the year rather than the first, and reveal the development of Radiguet's aesthetic interests. There is frequent use here of rhyme, and even of poetic fixed forms, including a sonnet ("Monologue," renamed "Victoire" in the later collection *Jeux Innocents*) and a rondel, "Nues" (Clouds). In addition, there are a number of parallels between Radiguet's poems and those by Cocteau from the same period.

The title *Couleurs sans danger* is taken from a poem, bearing the same name, in *Le Bonnet d'âne.* Radiguet must have been fond of this title, because he also uses it for one of the poems in *Couleurs sans danger.* It may well be borrowed from Jean Cocteau, who uses the expression in the first poem in his collection *Poésies 1917–1920* (1920) to describe the rainbow after a downpour, near his home in the suburbs of Paris:

CASE DE L'ONCLE TOM, les rampes et les herses
Du théâtre jadis me firent voyager

> Loin de notre jardin de banlieue où l'averse
> Fait fleurir l'arc-en-ciel aux couleurs sans danger
>
> (UNCLE TOM'S CABIN, the footlights and the battens
> Of the theater used to send me on a journey
> Far from our garden in the suburbs where the shower
> Brings out the rainbow with its harmless colors.)[19]

Drawing upon the notion of tranquillity after the storm—like the rainbow that appears when the rain has ceased—Radiguet may be making a reference, through his title, to the postwar period. This postwar brilliance may be contrasted with the dangerous colors of shells exploding during the war. These had been described by Apollinaire in poems such as "Merveilles de la guerre" (Wonders of war):

> Que c'est beau ces fusées qui illuminent la nuit
> Elles montent sur leur propre cime et se penchent pour regarder
> Ce sont des dames qui dansent avec leurs regards pour yeux bras et coeurs
>
> (How lovely are these rockets that light up the night
> They climb to their own summit then lean over to take a look
> They are ladies who dance with only gazes for eyes arms and hearts)[20]

Certainly the liminary poem "Prise d'armes" (Parade under arms) sets a tone of postwar lightheartedness, as it describes a parade on July 14, 1919, at which Henri Rousseau, the painter, hands out decorations:

> Bien en ordre, les soldats attendent le général qui doit distribuer des décorations
> Le général, c'est un peintre.
> Henri Rousseau, du bout de son pinceau, pose une étoile sur chaque poitrine
>
> (In fine array the soldiers await the general who is to hand out the decorations.
> The general is in fact a painter.
> Henri Rousseau, with the tip of his brush, places a star upon each chest.)[21]

The playfulness carries over into the individual poems in the collection. In "Joueuses de volant" (Badminton players), for example, the poet refers to his sisters' games. He had thought his sisters to be gentle, but as he watches them "killing" the shuttlecock, while they bat it to and fro, he is reminded of their teasing:

> Moi qui croyais a la douceur
>   De mes soeurs
> Mourez par excès de zèle
>   Timides oiselles
>   Dont le plumage meurti
>   Se rappelle les taquineries
>   De ces demoiselles (*OC*, 1:140)

> (I who believed in the gentleness
>   Of my sisters
> Die from [their] excessive zeal
>   Timid birdies
>   Whose bruised feathers
>   Remember the teasing
>   Of these girls)

A number of the images of *Couleurs sans danger,* including clay pipes, popular celebrations, fairs, as well as a mention of Paul and Virginie (characters in the novel of the same name by Bernardin de Saint-Pierre), are shared by Jean Cocteau in his volume *Poésies 1917–1920,* which appeared in 1920. The adoption of the fixed forms of the rondel or the sonnet suggests possible reading of Charles d'Orléans, Ronsard, or even of Cocteau's earliest poetry by Radiguet,[22] while elsewhere there is possibly some trace of an influence of Evaniste Parny.

In the poem entitled "Couleurs sans danger" the poet suggests some frolicking on the grass: "Gazon insoucieux de nos péchés comme par hasard au nombre de sept" ("Lawn heedless of our sins / which happen to number seven"). Radiguet came to make of grass or a lawn one of the staple elements of his personal landscape or mythology.[23] The image is present in slightly different but comparable form in Parny's poem "Au Gazon foulé par Eléonore" (To the lawn trodden upon by Eleonore); the poet requests of the lawn: "Of our lovers' trifling / Do not preserve the evidence: / You would cause too many to be jealous."[24] In sum, the influences on Radiguet's work still appeared to be very diverse indeed.

Radiguet and Cocteau: A Return to Convention

Radiguet's first published collection of poetry was the volume entitled *Les Joues en feu (Cheeks on Fire)*, which was brought out in 1920 by François Bernouard. Like the earlier manuscript poems, the fourteen pieces in this volume are diverse in character, ranging from a highly enigmatic "Le Langage des fleurs ou des étoiles" (The language of the flowers or the stars) to "Halte," which is remarkable for its visual, poster-like simplicity. The title itself suggests strong emotion coloring the cheeks, and the implication is that of love or sexual passion. The same title was used for the more copious volume, which was published after Radiguet's death. The image may have been suggested by Cocteau, who writes on several occasions, in his *Poésies 1917–1920,* of cheeks, and especially of red cheeks. Cocteau's fondness for the image probably derived in part from the pun in the expressions *Anjou* ("the province") and *en joue* ("aim!" in reference to placing one's cheek against the rifle butt). Cocteau's home address was of course 10, rue d'Anjou. At this time, moreover, Chénier was very much in vogue, since the centennial of the Latouche edition of Chénier had been celebrated in 1919. Radiguet was familiar with the work of Chénier; the eighteenth-century poet also makes frequent reference to crimson cheeks or flowering cheeks. And the image, suggestive of the color red, roundness, and love, is close in nature to that of the rose, dear to Ronsard and especially dear in 1920 to Cocteau, Radiguet, and their publisher Bernouard.[25]

When one abstracts from the 1920 *Joues en feu* those poems already to be found in *Le Bonnet d'âne, Couleurs sans danger,* and/or literary journals, what is left is slim indeed. Six of the fourteen pieces were to be retained moreover for the later, posthumous *Joues en feu.* This collection, on the other hand, is of great importance in appreciating Radiguet's qualities as a poet, and in tracing his evolution. To the extent that Radiguet is known at all as poet, it is largely thanks to the thirty-four poems to be found here.

Perhaps the most astonishing feature of the second *Joues en feu* is that it is in effect two collections in one. Radiguet affirms that the poems are presented in the chronological order of composition. Although Cocteau dated the first ones earlier, they in fact are from 1919. The poems from 1919 and 1920 are extremely diverse in nature and eclectic in inspiration. There is a greater reliance upon verse than ever before, but there is little pattern to the choice of verse: with ten-syllable terzarima in one poem ("Déjeuner de soleil" [The sun's lunch]), alexandrines in others ("Emploi du temps" [Time-table] and "Amélie"), and still other verse schemes in others. A number of these early poems are also in prose. While love is a major theme in these first poems of the collection, it is not the only one, and there are nature poems, and mention of fairs and childhood memories. The second, larger part of *Les Joues en feu* consists entirely of poems written in verse, in lines of eight syllables, usually rhymed, but not always. The inspiration of these poems centers largely upon the related themes of Venus and the sea. In the spring of 1921, Radiguet had fled to the fishing village of Carqueiranne, close to Toulon, in order to escape the frantic pace of life in Paris, and the stifling presence of Cocteau. In fact, after a separation of just three weeks, Cocteau joined Radiguet in the Midi. It was in these circumstances that Radiguet wrote his "regular" poems, while Cocteau, for his part, worked on the long poem about World War I, *Le Discours du grand sommeil* (The discourse on the long sleep).

Radiguet may well have been aware that the sharp contrast between the first poems in *Les Joues en feu* and the later, more classical pieces would leave an impression of unpleasant unevenness. Denying that he had been influenced by the shifting crosscurrents of the contemporary literary scene, from Max Jacob to Breton to Cocteau, Radiguet asserted instead that the obscurity of some of the early poems was the natural consequence of his adolescent shyness and reticence, while he inscribed the later ones in the tradition of the great French classical writers: ". . . it is Ronsard, Chénier, Malherbe, La Fontaine, Tristan L'Hermite who told me what poetry is."[26] Radiguet is less than frank, of course, in claiming to have been unaffected by his contemporaries, and especially in failing to mention Cocteau's name at all. In his correspondence at least, Cocteau took the credit for introducing a new, major theme into Radiguet's poetry: "Thanks to me Bébé [Radiguet] has become obsessed with death in his poems . . . ."[27] There is good reason to believe this to be true, judging by the emergence of this theme in some of the poems of *Les Joues en feu*.

Insofar as the principal theme of *Les Joues en feu*—although not the only one—is the youthful awakening to love, the first poem in the volume, entitled "Le Langage des fleurs ou des etoiles" (The language of flowers or stars), is entirely appropriate as a prologue or overture. Dated April 1919, it describes, in enigmatic terms, the narrator's encounter with twelve girls who resemble the months of the year. He is allowed to dance with them, but has no right to speak to them. On a rainy day, he offers the girls flowers, brought back from a journey. In summer, he and they count the stars in the sky. The poem closes on a note of considerable mystery, as a form of challenge to the reader: "The sky closes up again. You do not have a sharp enough ear." Written at the time that Radiguet was close to Jacob, and associating with the future surrealists, this poem has about it some of the mystery, even mystification, of the author of *Le Cornet à dés,* and the erotic interest of a poem by Breton. But it seems equally clear that Radiguet draws his inspiration from a more traditional source. In abbreviated and slightly modified form, "Le langage des fleurs ou des étoiles" is scarcely more than a retelling of the traditional fairy tale of the Twelve Dancing Princesses,[28] to be found in several different versions, including one by Grimm and another by the late-seventeenth-century French writer the Countess d'Aulnoy. In Mme d'Aulnoy's version, a boy called Michel, qualified by his contemporaries as the Star-Gazer, because he went about with his head in the air, won the hand of the youngest of twelve princesses who left their room each night to go dancing. The final line of Radiguet's poem, "You do not have a sharp enough ear," may be a mocking claim that the reader does not recognize this source, no more than the casual reader will perceive that, in a poem about twelve girls, the poem itself consists of twelve sentences!

The remaining poems, preceding the adoption of the octosyllabic line in 1921, tend to be short and lighthearted. While they are not profound, they are cleverly executed, and there has been a tendency to underestimate their skill in order better to concentrate upon the later, "regular" pieces, which corroborate the image of a "classical" Radiguet.

"Tombola," dated July 1919, has some of the melancholy of the fairground that Radiguet credited to Cocteau.

On dirait la Grande Roue.

        Une broche à l'heureux gagnant; le pauvre marin, ne sachant qu'en faire, de rage pique au vif l'azur de son béret, et, à défaut d'un prénom de femme, y fait inscrire celui de son bateau.

—Où puis-je avoir laissé mon éventail?
—Vous ne voyez pas d'ici? Il fait la roue, sur la pelouse, où des trèfles à quatre feuilles poussent en cachette.

Les jeunes filles qui montent en balançoire rougissent chacune à leur tour:
leurs robes blanches s'accrochent aux bras de l'épouvantail.
—Elles aussi sont toutes rouges, les cerises.
Sans faire de jalouses, le galant épouvantail offre des boucles d'oreilles.

Le pauvre marin ne possède d'autre bijou qu'une broche, gagnée à la
tombola. (*OC,* 1:25–26)

As happens so often, Radiguet states his theme in the first line: "It
looks like the Ferris Wheel." The remainder of the poem explores
variations upon this image of movement. The spinning of the wheel
of fortune brings a sailor luck: he wins a brooch, but having no girl
friend to whom to offer it, he has the name of his ship engraved
upon it. The scene shifts slightly to a conversation, overhead, as a
girl asks: "—Where can I have left my fan?" The answer given also
provides an image of circular movement: "—Don't you see it from
here? It is turning cartwheels, on the lawn, where four-leafed clovers
grow in secret." The image that follows, that of girls on a swing,
was almost an obsession of Radiguet's, and recalls the earlier images
of motion in this poem; as they swing, they appear to fly into the
arms of a scarecrow in the background, standing guard over an
orchard of cherries. And the scarecrow, as the result of an optical
illusion, appears to offer the girls earrings—his cherries:

The girls who go up on the swing blush, each in turn: their white dresses
get caught on the arms of the scarecrow.

—They too are all red, these cherries.
Without making any of the girls jealous, the gallant scarecrow makes a
gift of earrings.

The conclusion of the poem takes us back to the point of departure,
the poor sailor, whose only jewel is the brooch he has won in the
lottery.

   A sense of playfulness pervades these poems from 1919 to 1920.
They are relatively untroubled by profound concerns of any sort. In
"Une Carte Postale: Les quais de Paris" (A post card: the embank-
ments of Paris), for example, the poet offers a picturesque image of
the Seine as a river from which seashells have now disappeared,
giving way, in modern times, to booksellers, along the banks. To
be sure, playing upon the pun in the words *ancre/encre* ("anchor/

ink"), and making reference to his own profession as a writer, the poet claims that his craft[29] is a sad one, and he wishes to leave. But the words are so obviously a pastiche of Mallarmé's poem "Brise Marine" (Sea breeze):

> La chair est triste, hélas! et j'ai lu tous les livres.
>
> Je partirai! Steamer balancant ta mâture,
> Lève l'ancre pour une exotique nature!
>
> (The flesh is sad, alas, and I have read all the books.
>
> I shall leave! Steamer with your swaying masts,
> Weigh anchor, sail for an exotic nature!)[30]

that we cannot take them very seriously and they leave an impression of carefree composition:

> On a remplacé les coquillages
> Par des boîtes à livres. J'appris
> Qu'il est de bien plus jolis rivages
> En feuilletant les livres de prix.
>
> Cher ami, sans retard levons l'ancre;
> Encrier triste comme la mer.
> De grâce, n'écrivez plus à l'encre
> Les mots qu'on y pêche sont amers. (*OC*, 1:25–26)
>
> (They have replaced the shells
> With book-boxes. I learned
> Of much prettier shores
> On leafing through books won as prizes.
>
> Dear friend, let's tarry no more and weigh anchor;
> Ink-well, sad as is the sea
> Pray, write no more in ink
> The words we fish from it are bitter.)

Even more lighthearted, like a poster from the Belle Epoque, is the very short poem "Halte," depicting a girl cyclist. She seems arrested in time, as if in a painting or drawing, but is encouraged to keep up her pace—it is the French tradition to overcome obsta-

cles—in spite of the temptation to rest, or take time out for love.
The subject is announced in the first line:

> Cycliste en jupe-culotte!
> A travers tous les ages, la route nationale mollement se déroule,
> comme ta bande molletière.
> Le culte des obstacles est en honneur chez nos ancêtres gaulois: pour-
> suis le petit bonhomme des chemins, malgré la borne kilométrique qui
> t'invite à la fatigue, au repos de l'amour. (*OC,* 1:36)

> (Cyclist in a divided skirt!
> Throughout the ages, the highway leisurely unwinds, like your anklets.
> Our Gaulish ancestors are devoted to defying obstacles: keep plodding
> along, in spite of the milestone, inviting you to take a break for the fatigue
> and the repose of love.)

The image of the girl cyclist presumably had special significance
for Radiguet, since a girl in a divided skirt is also the subject of
one of his obscene poems, set in Joinville, close to Radiguet's home
at Saint-Maur.[31] Cocteau also made use of the cyclist in his poetry,
in "Contrebande" (Contraband) of *Vocabulaire,* the 1922 collection:
"Pédale, / Cycliste rose!" ("Pedal, / Pink cyclist!").
   "Halte" is dated May 1920, and was first published in *Le Coq.*
So rapid was Radiguet's development—a few months in his life
were comparable, in the developments they brought, to several years
in another writer's—that "Automne," an irregular sonnet from December 1920, has little in common with his earlier poems. It is
one of his most beautiful pieces.

> Tu le sais, inimitable fraise des bois
> Comme un charbon ardente aux doigts de qui te cueille:
>   Leçons et rires buissonniers
>   Ne se commandent pas.
>   Chez le chasseur qui la met en joue
> L'automne pense-t-elle susciter l'émoi
> Que nous mettent au coeur les plus jeunes mois?
>   Blessée à mort, Nature,
>   Et feignant encore
>   D'une Eve enfantine la joue
> Que fardent non la pudeur mais les confitures,
>   Ta mûre témérité
>   S'efforce de mériter

> La feuille de vigne vierge. (*OC,* 1:40)

It starts with the striking image of a wild strawberry, which is "Like a blazing coal in the fingers of the person who picks it." The color and ripeness of the strawberry are inimitable and cannot be obtained through an effort of will. By the same token, the poet asserts, turning to the withering of life that takes place in autumn, nature cannot preserve its vitality and youth with the disappearance of the summer. Its fruits lend it color, but this is not the color of the bloom of spring, but rather a cosmetic concealment of impending death:

> Mortally wounded, Nature
> And while you still feign
> The rosy cheek of a youthful Eve
> Your cheek is brightened not by modesty but fruit preserves,
> Your temerity, acquired with ripe old age
> Strives to merit
> The grape-leaf accorded to the cradle.

The Birth of Desire

In the foreword he prepared for his collected poems, Radiguet claimed some credit for shedding light, in *Les Joues en feu,* on a little-described experience:

Les Joues en feu will perhaps be able to illuminate a particularly mysterious minute: the birth of Venus, which must not be confused with the birth of Love. It is before or after our heart that our senses awaken: never at the same time. (*OC,* 1:17)

The birth of desire is not the only theme to be treated in the regular, octosyllabic verse, which makes up more than half—the second part—of *Les Joues en feu*. But it is the major one. In some cases, it emerges in a pattern of circumstances wholly reminiscent of Radiguet's earlier poetry. "Le Rendezvous solitaire," for example, is an elaboration, in verse, of "Halte." A girl cyclist is now encouraged to linger in a leafy arbor:

> Emprunte aux oiseaux leur auberge
> Au feuillage d'ardoise tendre!

> Loin des fatigues, ma cycliste,
> Qui t'épanouis sur nos berges.
> Future fleur comme Narcisse,
>
> Tu sembles toi-même t'attendre.
> Mais pour que nul gêneur ne vienne,
> Je nomme la Marne gardienne,
> O peu chaste, de tes appas.
> La Marne fera les cent pas. (*OC,* 1:44)
>
> (Borrow from the birds their inn
> With its foliage of tender slate!
> Far from fatigue, my cyclist!
> You blossom on our banks.
> A future flower, like Narcissus,
>
> You seem to be awaiting no one but yourself.
> So to ensure that no intruder can appear
> I appoint the Marne guardian,
> Albeit unchaste, of your charms.
> The Marne will stand watch.)

The Marne River is named guardian of her charms. But appearances are deceptive; its wish, as much as the poet's, is to have the girl experience passion:

> Si son eau douce va semblant
> Plus douce et plus chaste que d'autres,
> Ses désirs pourtant sont les nôtres:
> Voir bouillir à l'heure du thé
> Que l'on prend en pantalon blanc,
>
> Au soleil, ta virginité.
>
> (If its fresh water, in flowing along
> Seems gentler and more chaste than others,
> Its desires are still the same as ours:
> To see come to a boil when it's time for tea
> Which is taken in white dress pants
>
> In the sunshine, your virginity.)

While earlier motifs remain, and one cannot simply divorce this section of Radiguet's poetry from his earlier production, there is a pattern of convergence that had been less noticeable before. All of these twenty poems are composed in the traditional verse of the French lyric or ode, the octosyllable, common to Charles d'Orléans, Tristan L'Hermite, Parny, and many others. But these pieces are traditional in other respects, too, since they choose to represent the birth of love in the conventional, classical guise of the birth of Venus. In writing near the Mediterranean, Radiguet appears to have discovered the meaning of this myth, as well as the importance of its Mediterranean setting. Venus, the sea, the shepherd boy, and the nymph form a cluster of classical motifs that are particularly striking here. It may well be that at this time Radiguet, having opted for a "classical" or conservative aesthetic, adopted it completely in his poetry and turned his back upon the pursuit of novelty.

If the poems themselves are to be relied upon as accurate testimony, Radiguet underwent a change in viewing the Mediterranean. He learned for the first time to "read" or understand the sea:

> Vénus non seulement me livre
> Ses secrets, mais ceux de sa mère:
> Jadis je regardais la mer
> Comme regarderait les livres
>
> Un enfant qui ne sait pas lire.[32]
>
> (Venus not only delivers up to me
> Her secrets but those of her mother:
> Formerly I would look at the sea
> As would look at a book
>
> A child who does not know how to read.)

Elsewhere, reflecting upon Venus's itinerary—born in the sea, then rising to heaven, to her "hammock" in the star of Venus—the poet expresses his desire not to have a resting place in the sky; instead, he would prefer the sea, where she was born:

> Ne me promets ton paradis,
> Mais, dans les Méditerranées,
> De dormir où Vénus est née.[33]
>
> (Do not promise me your paradise,

But, in the Mediterraneans,
To sleep where Venus was born.)

Death and the Angel

One of the most obvious results of the close contact between
Radiguet and Cocteau in the spring of 1921 was the emergence of
the associated themes of death and a supernatural angel. The two
are found of course in Cocteau's work. In 1921, Cocteau was busy
putting the final touches to his long poem *Le Discours du grand
sommeil,* in which a principal theme—the "Long Sleep" of the title—
is death, and the main protagonist, a kind of personified conscience,
summoning the poet to his duty, is an angel. Cocteau's angel in *Le
Discours du grand sommeil* is comparable to Rilke's in the *Duino Elegies.*
It is mysterious, remote, and inscrutable, a creature dwelling within
the poet's own depths. It assumes the role of guide, embodying the
principles of direction and guardianship. It has as its mission to
lead the poet into the unknown, far from the city:

> Cet ange me dit: Pars
> Que fais-tu entre les remparts de ta ville?
> . . . .
> Va et raconte
> l'homme tout nu,
> tout vêtu de ce qu'il trouve
> dans sa caverne,
>
> (This angel bids me: Depart
> What are you doing within the ramparts of your city?
> . . . .
> Go and recount
> man in his nakedness,
> dressed simply in what he finds
> in his cave.)[34]

The angel remained a stellar figure in Cocteau's personal mythology,
especially filling the whole of the long poem "L'Ange Heurtebise"
(1925), heavily influenced by the death of Radiguet. Radiguet's
poem "L'Ange" may well have influenced the development of Cocteau's own angels. Like those of Cocteau, Radiguet's angel has little
in common with those of Christianity. It comes into this world and,
having tried to understand the laws that govern it, becomes its

prisoner and is forced to remain on earth. First, unwittingly, it puts a large snowball in its pocket, and is then unable to take off. It remains "Among us the earthly convicts." Things go from bad to worse; beating its wings, struggling to escape, it falls among chestnut trees, where its hair is caught in the resin and it is entrapped more than ever. In a final stanza, which, like a number of other parts of the poem, anticipates "L'Ange Heurtebise," it is led off to prison by two gendarmes.

The angel reappears in the final poem of the collection, "Un Cygne Mort . . ." (A dead swan . . .), where it comes into the world and then, leaving no trace, is able to depart it. The principal image of the poem, however, is that of the dead swan itself, dear to many writers, including Chénier, Mallarmé, and Cocteau. One of the poems in Cocteau's volume *Vocabulaire* is called "Mort d'un cygne" (Death of a swan), and the conclusion to this "swansong," in which the bird, about to die, says it will soon be indistinguishable from the foam of the waves,

> Onde cruelle à qui je plus,
> Ouvre ton éventail de plumes
> Déjà je fonds, je suis écume . . .
> Bientôt je ne chanterai plus.[35]

> (Cruel wave whom once I pleased,
> Open up your fan of feathers
> Already I melt, I am foam . . .
> Soon I shall no longer sing.)

is close indeed to the first lines of Radiguet's piece:

> Un cygne mort ne se remarque
> Parmi l'écume au bord du lac. (*OC,* 1:81)

> (A dead swan is not noticed
> Among the foam at the lake's edge.)

This new, somber note in Radiguet's poetry may well, as Cocteau claimed, have been owed to the older poet. In any case, like Cocteau in *Vocabulaire,* Radiguet evokes the theme of death in a number of poems. In "Elégie" it is touched upon rather lightly:

> Mais les anges sont des ténors
> Se ménageant pour chanter haut
> Notre louange, dès la mort. (*OC*, 1:74)

> (But angels are tenors
> Sparing themselves so as to sing out loud
> Our praises, when we die.)

In "Fragment d'une élégie," the emphasis remains upon the glory that will surround the poet's name after his death, and the fear of death itself is decried:

> La peur de mourir, mon beau cygne,
> A ton chant ôte sa beauté. (*OC*, 1:80)

> (The fear of dying, my lovely swan,
> Detracts from the beauty of your song.)

And death is the theme of "Avec la mort tu te maries . . ." (With death you are wed . . .). While the poem is hardly profound, the insistence upon the subject of death suggests a new departure, a new seriousness, in Radiguet's thinking, at a time when, without question, Cocteau, for his part, having turned thirty, was aware that a serious sense of purpose had been rather lacking in his production up to that time. Radiguet suggests, in the first lines of his poem, that death has entered his life and changed his condition. He is quick to insist, however, that he means living with death, not putting an end to life:

> Avec la mort tu te maries
> Sans le consentement des dieux;
> Mais le suicide est tricherie
> Qui nous rend aux joueurs odieux,
> De leur ciel nous fermant la porte. (*OC*, 1:77)

> (With death you are wed
> Without the consent of the gods;
> But suicide is cheating
> Which makes us odious in the eyes of the players,
> Shutting the gate of their heaven in our face.)

"Avec la mort tu te maries . . ." is one of two poems by Radiguet included in André Gide's anthology of French poets (1949); indeed, poems by Radiguet close this collection.[36] It would be a considerable overstatement to claim that Radiguet is known as a poet thanks to this inclusion. In fact he is still scarcely known as a poet, since his reputation as a novelist greatly overshadowed his other literary career. But there is no doubt that, to the extent that Radiguet the poet is known at all, it is for his regular, octosyllabic verse, and the Gide anthology helped remind readers that Radiguet was more than a novelist.

Conclusion: Radiguet's Status as Poet

If one takes into consideration all of Radiguet's production as a poet—those poems published during his lifetime, and the many others that appeared subsequently, from the erotic pieces, to a brief 1926 collection called *Jeux Innocents* (Innocent games), to a substantial manuscript collection presented to the public in 1959, in the *Complete Works*—the total volume is very impressive, and all the more so if one recalls that the poems date essentially from the first years of Radiguet's career as a writer: from 1918 until about 1921. Mirrored here are a number of artistic trends and temptations in this most creative of periods; Reverdy, Apollinaire, Jacob, the *Esprit Nouveau,* cubism, dada—all are reflected in Radiguet's poems. In the company of Cocteau, Radiguet then chose a different direction, opting for more conventional, classical models, and his work came to bear the imprint of Charles d'Orléans, Ronsard, Tristan l'Hermite, Parny, and Chénier—and of course Cocteau himself.

The question of Radiguet's authenticity needs to be posed, but an answer is elusive. To what extent is the voice that speaks through his poems his own? One must concede that the influences upon him are numerous and frequently obvious. They may even be greater than has commonly been realized. One critic has shown that one brief, unpublished piece, first presented in the *Complete Works,* is in fact the transcription by Radiguet of lines by Chénier that apparently pleased him.[37] Elsewhere, the presence of Tristan l'Hermite seems rather evident. Quite apart from the images of Venus and the sea and the stars, common to both Tristan and Radiguet, a more specific influence may on occasion be detected, as when Radiguet talks of the fisherman caught in his own nets—the nets of love—an image commonly employed by Tristan.[38] Tristan l'Hermite's *Le Promenoir des deux amants* (The promenade of the two lovers) was of course published by Bernouard, a publisher of both Cocteau and Radiguet, who encouraged them in their return to classical models.

Cocteau took pleasure in affirming Radiguet's influence upon him. The actual situation, it seems clear, was not nearly so simple. It seems true that Radiguet's preferred books were of a more elevated stature than Cocteau's, and that even when very young Radiguet enjoyed the French classics. So it is possible that Radiguet did indeed introduce his protector to some serious writers. On the other hand, the two authors' adoption of "classicism" around 1920 or 1921 was by no means the work of Radiguet alone. The "return to the rose" was for Cocteau no more than a re-adoption of an aesthetic position that had been his ten years or so earlier! The poems of *La Lampe d'Aladin* (1909), *Le Prince Frivole* (1910), and *La Danse de Sophocle* (1912), while wan in their presentation of moonlit scenes, deserted gardens, and lingering melancholy, present many of the features, including lots of roses, later to be adopted by Radiguet and re-adopted by Cocteau. As in Radiguet's work, one can find here sonnets and rondels, and a number of figures—Marie-Antoinette, Narcissus, Venus, Paul et Virginie—later to be featured by Radiguet. Long before Radiguet sang the praises of the Ile-de-France or the Marne region, Cocteau wrote of *his* love for the Seine-et-Oise:

> Pas un pays lointain ne vaut
> Ce jardinet de Seine-et-Oise[39]

> (No, not any distant land is a match for
> This little garden of Seine-et-Oise)

When one compares Cocteau's poems in *Poésies 1917–1920* and *Vocabulaire* (1922) with many of Radiguet's pieces from the same period, there are indeed many similarities. Their defense of tradition, classicism, Ronsard, and du Bellay may appear daring in a time of avant-garde ferment. But it is worth recalling that this adoption of tradition was, in effect, for Cocteau a "second time around." This time, to be sure, Cocteau displays little of the consumptive symbolist languor that had marked his first collections. Radiguet, for his part, was not entirely immune to it. In 1909 Cocteau had published in *La Lampe d'Aladin* a poem called "Le Problème," which, lachrymose and nocturnal, is rather typical of the collection but astonishing in comparison to Cocteau's later, "avant-garde" poetry. "The Problem"

of the title is that of trying to understand the death of four roses
(!) in an earthenware bowl:

Quatre roses mouraient dans la vasque en faïence
. . . .
Tout semblait dans la nuit s'émouvoir et se tendre,
Tout criait son regret à la mort de ces fleurs,
. . . .
Et tout avait une âme et tout avait des pleurs!
. . . .
Les objets réunis s'effaraient du problème
Grave et mystérieux de comprendre pourquoi.[40]

(Four roses were dying in the earthenware bowl
. . . .
In the dark everything seemed to be moved and to reach out,
. . . .
Everything called its regret at the death of these flowers,
. . . .
And everything had a soul, everything had tears!
. . . .
The gathered objects were startled at that problem,
Grave and mysterious, of understanding why.)

Among Radiguet's unpublished manuscripts was found a poem entitled "Sur la mort d'une rose," published in 1973, which is astonishingly similar to Cocteau's piece. Here, it is one rose, not four,
in a clay vase, not an earthenware bowl. But the thought expressed
is identical:

Cette rose qui meurt dans un vase d'argile
Attriste mon regard,
Elle paraît souffrir et son fardeau fragile
Sera bientôt épars.

Les pétales tombés dessinent sur la table
Une couronne d'or,
Et pourtant un parfum subtil et palatable
Vient me troubler encore.[41]

(This rose which is dying in a clay vase
Saddens my gaze,

It appears to suffer and its fragile burden
Will soon be scattered.

The fallen petals form on the table
A crown of gold,
And yet a fragrance, subtle though perceptible
Remains to trouble me still.)

If indeed the poem is by Radiguet as has been claimed, and not by
Cocteau, it is one more indication—of which there are already
many—that the influence of Cocteau on his protégé was far greater
than he was ever willing to concede.

Any attempt to understand what kind of poet Radiguet might
have become if he had survived is very difficult and exceedingly
speculative. A number of motifs did recur in his work—water, sky,
wind, and stars; grass and lawns; Venus and girls—and these suggest
the nucleus of a poetic vision that might "settle" and achieve some
constancy. Nonetheless we retain the impression not of a coherent
poetic *oeuvre,* but rather of many different individual poems, reaching
out in various directions. Radiguet was not a great poet, translating
a deeply held, compulsive vision. Nonetheless, his poems, well
crafted, intrinsically engaging, and remarkable also as a record of
influences, deserve to be much better known than has been their
fate up to the present.

Chapter Three
Devil in the Flesh
Background

The years immediately following World War I, and continuing into the early 1920s, leave an impression of life led at a frantic pace, and of artistic movements pulling energetically, exorbitantly, and with great clamor in a number of different directions. Many traditional values—church and country, family, class, and tradition itself—had been weakened, in the opinion of a large number of Frenchmen, by the horrendous casualties of the war and the perceived senselessness of much of the destruction. Even a writer as traditional as François Mauriac recognized that, in a relatively godless age, it would be difficult and dishonest to write works centered upon religious conflict. He praised the sincerity of authors who recognized this as a period of *crisis* in literature.[1]

It was from the soil of bankrupt values that first dada and then surrealism were to grow. Breton, the founder of surrealism, was very lucid in understanding that an era had passed, and in striving to banish its last vestiges. One small aspect of this view was his perception that the novel, as genre, implied a stable world order, coherence, and progression, the division of reality into subordinate and superordinate categories: a total scheme in which he and his associates found it impossible to believe. Breton's response was to attack the realist novel, with its dependence on logic, and to deny the possibility of legitimately writing one in an age of disorder and transition. In Breton's opinion, only a narrative dependent upon illogic, the irrational, and the extraordinary was admissible:

In the realm of literature, only the marvelous is capable of fecundating works which belong to an inferior category such as the novel, and generally speaking anything that involves storytelling. Lewis' *The Monk* is an admirable proof of this. It is infused throughout with the presence of the marvelous. Long before the author has freed his main characters from all temporal constraints, one feels them ready to act with an unprecedented pride. This passion for eternity with which they are constantly stirred lends an unforgettable intensity to their torments, and to mine.[2]

Around 1919 and 1920, Cocteau and Radiguet at least seemed to stand shoulder to shoulder with the avant-garde. They appeared to be part of the "rowdy demonstrations and the agitated lectures"[3] that attacted the attention, resentment, or the scorn of the press. Shock and confusion appeared to be worthwhile objectives to be pursued by the avant-garde. Complacency was the enemy. Pierre Reverdy's lapidary aphorisms in *Self-Defence* (1919) seem to belong in an old tradition of French moralists' reflections on art and life. But their message expresses younger artists' yearning to break free of prevailing tastes and recognize the complexity of reality: "The duration of a work's interest is in direct proportion to the quantity of inexplicable it contains"; "the first are often last. Mediocrity always recognizes its own"; "he who mingles with the crowd shares its attitude and way of seeing things."[4]

Aligned against the avant-garde, but by no means in serried ranks, more traditional artists still stood, a rearguard action, eager to be counted and to prevail. Following in the footsteps of Paul Bourget, Anatole France, or Maurice Barrès, a number of writers would stress, in the immediate postwar period, the anxiety that afflicted the generation. Just as sincerity was a key term, so too was anxiety. Chadourne's novel *L'Inquiète Adolescence* (Anxious adolescence) and Obey's, *L'Enfant Inquiet* (The anxious child), are just two among many that capture this mood. So, even the more traditional writers were aware that the world was no longer the place of security it had once appeared to be. But these writers, whether on the right or left, shared with the many regional writers, or a number of others who wrote about the war, the belief that something could be salvaged from recent events: that there was some redeeming meaning, some transcendent, positive value to be discovered.

The casualties of the Great War had been appalling: 17.6 percent of the French soldiers were killed. This represented more than 10 percent of France's active male population. Three million soldiers were wounded. These were the highest losses France had ever sustained. At the same time that young survivors with young ideas demanded radical change, old men with prewar ideas were swept into power; in 1919 the first right-wing, conservative parliament was elected since the formation of the Third Republic.[5]

The journalists and critics of the period were very much aware of the crisis in values, and of the differing responses to it. Some comparison was made with the romantic period of French history, the time around 1820 to 1830. Emile Henriot summed up this viewpoint in an article in the *Revue de Paris* in June 1920: "For you are not unaware that the struggle between classicism and romanticism is almost as lively as it was a century ago."[6]

Reception

It was against this background that Radiguet's novel *Le Diable au corps (Devil in the Flesh)* appeared in March 1923. It was railed against by Breton and the *Littérature* group,[7] who had abandoned dada the year before (in 1922) and were about to found surrealism. They could not countenance Radiguet's proximity to Cocteau or his composition of a traditional novel. On the other hand, as a novel about the war, in which a valiant French soldier is cuckolded by a young upstart while *he* is fighting at the front, it was criticized, as was inevitable, by others who were totally out of sympathy with André Breton. Rather astonishingly, Radiguet sent a copy of the work to Roland Dorgelès, who was himself the author of *Les Croix de bois* (Wooden crosses, 1919). This was the most popular of the novels about the war, and had been received most sympathetically by a public that had no difficulty in identifying with the protagonists, soldiers at the front, living in the mud of the trenches, surrounded and constantly threatened by mutilation and death. These soldiers cannot help being utterly dismayed by that lack of understanding of what they have been through, displayed by the civilians who have stayed home and seen none of the atrocity of the war. The reader is shown from close up the physical pain and mental anguish of the protagonist, Sulphart, who is wounded and then, in the hospital, longing for letters from his wife, receives only brief, impersonal, infrequent notes. On the very day that he learns that he has earned a discharge from the army, his joy is cut short by a letter from his *concierge,* informing him that his wife has run off with a Belgian, taking all of their furniture with her. Dorgelès spares no detail of the suffering brought on by the war. But the suffering does finally end. The final chapter expresses a sense of gratitude, in spite of everything, that for some at least life does resume:

Now it's over . . .

Here is the sheet of paper on the table, the peaceful lamp and the books. . . . Who would have believed we would ever see them again, when we were down there, so far removed from home?

We used to speak of our life as of a dead thing, the certainty of never coming back again separated us from it like a limitless sea and hope itself seemed to grow small, limiting the desire strictly to surviving until we were relieved. There were too many shells, too many dead, too many crosses; sooner or later our turn had to come.

And yet it's over now . . .

Life will resume its happy course. The horrible memories which still torment us will die down, we will forget, and the time may come when, equating war with the passing of youth, we shall heave a sigh of regret when we think of those years.[8]

Dorgelès replied politely to Radiguet, thanking him for sending the book, but could not help deploring the young writer's "absolute lack of heart." Complaining of the mishandling of the soldier Jacques, cuckolded by the adolescent narrator, Dorgelès allowed himself a complaint alongside a compliment: "In your novel, in which I do recognize profound qualities, I looked in vain for one expression of regret, one instant of emotion, one vague sign of remorse . . . this I did not find."[9] A number of critics could not fail to be offended by Radiguet's peculiar child's-eye view of the war, given on the very first page:

I am going to leave myself open to many reproaches. Yet what can I do about it? Is it my fault if I had my twelfth birthday a few months before the declaration of war? No doubt the troubles that overcame me in this extraordinary period were of a kind that one never experiences at this age: but as there is no force strong enough to make us old before our years, in spite of appearances, it is as a child that I was to conduct myself in an adventure which would have given a grown man trouble in knowing what to do. I am not the only one. And my companions will have a memory of this era which is not that of their elders. Let those who nurse a grudge against me consider what the war was for so many young boys: a four-year summer holiday.[10]

Even those who were not offended by the substance of the book deplored Grasset's all-out publicity campaign, which struck them as unseemly.

Certainly Grasset had a well-deserved reputation for being adept at gaining as much exposure as possible for the books of his young writers. Radiguet seems to have been happy to be so well publicized, even though Cocteau claimed on one occasion that "he put up with Grasset's advertising out of tact, out of gratitude for the sums which supported his father, mother, and six brothers and sisters."[11] Max Jacob recognized that times had changed, and that it had now become necessary to "sell" writers to the public; in this perception as in so many others, Jacob was ahead of his time: "This is no longer the time of shade-loving flowers in dark churches, it is the century of publicity. Shall we do less for art and faith than Cadum for its soap?"[12]

Radiguet was referred to as the "Cadum Baby" by Grasset, who, even before the publication of *Devil in the Flesh*, carefully courted leading Parisian critics, sending them and other important person-alities galleys for the novel, with a letter:

I am delighted to recommend to you the galleys of a novel that I am about to publish which has as its title *Devil in the Flesh*. Its author, Raymond Radiguet, was scarcely seventeen when he wrote this novel. I do not believe that since Rimbaud, who at this age had completed his po-etic works, we have been faced with such a literary phenomenon. . . . [13]

While seeking maximum exposure, Grasset played down the book's "shocking" side:

Devil in the Flesh is the book of a child who finds himself locked in a man's adventure and analyzes himself with miraculous clairvoyance, with-out false modesty or hypocrisy.

It is also war seen with the eyes of a child and this is so novel that, from this point of view alone, Radiguet's book strikes me as deserving a place in contemporary literature.

Only those persons who consider *Daphnis and Chloé* a libertine novel will perhaps be shocked by *Devil in the Flesh*. It is the charming immodesty of childhood and all its secret mechanisms shown in broad daylight by a Master of seventeen.[14]

But there can be no possible doubt that Grasset's publicity campaign was extraordinary by the standards of the day. The book was sold in train stations, Radiguet's photograph looked out from the windows of bookstores throughout the country, and even in the movies Radiguet and Grasset were to be seen: "for a whole week the cinema newsreels showed Grasset seated nobly at his desk, signing with a grand gesture the first check for 100,000 francs to have been presented by a French publisher to a young author and recorded on film."[15]

Max Jacob, eager to please his friends Radiguet and Cocteau, still expressed his fear that the work might be "antireligious . . . sadistic, immodest, dreadful."[16] While Mauriac praised it, seeing the presentation of innocents caught up in the situation not of their making, and Kemp compared it favorably to *Les Liaisons Dangereuses* by Laclos, others, including Souday in *Le Mot,* pointed to careless features of the style, including spelling errors.[17]

The storm surrounding *Devil in the Flesh* blew up anew when it was learned that many of the elements that when into it were indeed autobiographical. We now know that Radiguet had had an affair with a young woman named Alice, whose husband was in the war, and this in 1917, when the author was fourteen years of age! André Salmon later recounted speaking with the young woman, who lived close to Radiguet's parents, in Montmartre, after she had been "dropped" by Radiguet. It is said even that she had a child by him. The unfortunate husband took his story or version of events to Roland Dorgelès.

The provocative character of the novel and of the circumstances attending its publication did not of course hurt sales; on the contrary. All of the literary columns presented articles devoted to *Devil in the Flesh.* There were more than thirty within a month of its appearance. A first printing of six thousand copies had to be followed up within a week by another, of ten thousand. By the end of one month, more than forty-one thousand copies had been printed. Sales continue to be solid, if not spectacular, having reached a total of close to two hundred thousand in France.

Analysis: Time, Space, and the River

The story told in *Devil in the Flesh* is simple and even banal. It describes the circumstances leading up to, in the course of, and following a love affair between the unnamed first-person narrator, who is a mere youth, and his mistress, Marthe. Marthe is three years older than he. She marries Jacques, a soldier at the front, whom she scarcely knows, and with whom she does not find happiness. The liaison is conducted in the Marne region, specifically in the *départements* of Seine, Seine and Marne, and Seine and Oise, as well as in Paris. The events described go from the narrator's childhood, when he is twelve, in March 1914, until a few months after the Armistice, around March 1919. The end of the war brings the end of the liaison, and also the death of Marthe in childbirth. The husband assumes that this son—fathered in fact by the narrator—is his own. The narrator, saddened but wiser, detects some pattern to life as he views Jacques:

> I wished to see the man to whom Marthe had pledged her troth.
> Holding my breath and walking on tiptoe, I made for the open door. I got there just in time to hear:
> "My wife died calling his name. Poor child! Isn't he my only reason for living?"
> Upon seeing the dignity of this widower, and how he mastered his grief, I understood that in the long run order takes care of things. Hadn't I just learned that Marthe had died calling my name, and that my son would have an orderly existence. (*D*, 456)

Radiguet himself expressed strong feelings of distaste for the nineteenth century and in particular for the realist movement. But there is about *Devil in the Flesh* an appearance of truth; it gives an impression of experience lived, of verisimilitude. It is true that the story provides little information about material circumstances such as income earned, clothes worn, height, weight, or appearance of the principal protagonists: in other words Radiguet does not present his characters in the detailed manner of a Stendhal or a Balzac, let alone a Zola. He appears to respect his own intention, which was to subordinate all of the material conditions of the tale to the treatment of love. In this respect, he returns to a tradition that goes back to the seventeenth century, but which has been followed by other later writers also, including talents as diverse as Laclos, Benjamin Constant, and Eugène Fromentin, whose works Radiguet knew. One must therefore ask, in the face of the remarkable paucity of detail—absolutely no description of how the narrator looks, no mention of his name and, similarly, very few details indeed about Marthe's appearance—what it is that gives this work such a ring of truth, such an air of authenticity.

There is, in the first place, a very effective and astute presentation of both space and time in *Devil in the Flesh* and these combine to thrust the reader into a three-dimensional world that successfully imitates reality. The names of places, all located in a well-defined, specific geographic area, press upon us. La Varenne, Chennevières, Ormesson, Sucy, Lagny, Meaux, Brunoy, Mandres all appear, then reappear or disappear, described briefly, but with just enough accuracy and telling appropriateness to give weight and credibility to the action. We learn, for example, that the narrator would go with his companions and play his mischievous games "upon the slopes of Chennevières" (*D,* 305). This may be the sketchiest of descriptions; but like all the others, it is accurate; Chennevières's most distinctive characteristic is that it does stand relatively high on a plateau, looking down upon the Marne. Elsewhere, the narrator expresses his dream of staying in Mandres, with Marthe, because it is a town where roses are grown, and, every night, a train leaves there, with a load of the flowers; this image had always fired his imagination (*D,* 410). This may seem irrelevant. But it is not. It rings true, if one realizes that the full name of Mandres—never spelled out in *Devil in the Flesh*—is in fact Mandres-les-Roses. It is not of course in any single, brief description that Radiguet endows his narrative with a substantive, substantial background. It is rather in the accumulation of such brief notations that he provides what Stendhal called "little, true facts" forming a coherent and convincing overall picture. Even in the case of two towns the names of which are not given, Radiguet effectively gives an impression of authenticity. The two are identified simply as F . . . and J. . . . One obvious reason for their being presented only by initial letters is that Radiguet wishes to give the impression of protecting the identity of the two protagonists in this love story. The narrator lives in F . . ., while Marthe's home is in J. . . . In fact, however, if one really wishes to identify their real-life, geographic counterparts, they appear to exist: Parc Saint-Maur (F . . .) and Champigny (J . . .). A number of details given in the novel seem to indicate these two towns. They are two kilometers apart, there is a railway bridge at Champigny, and the military trains passed by there during the war.

Perhaps the single most effective technique used by Radiguet to reinforce the impression of verisimilitude is the constantly mentioned, ineluctable presence of the Marne, the river itself, acting as an effective counterpoint to the foreground events and action. We have the impression that it is always there, flowing gently, a kind of muted commentary. When the narrator witnesses a death and faints, his father takes him to the Marne to recover: ". . . he bore me off to the edge of the Marne. We remained there very late, in silence, lying in the grass" (*D*, 303). Here is the first mention of the narrator's hometown: "We lived in F . . . on the banks of the Marne" (*D*, 290) and of Marthe's house: "Marthe lived in J . . ., her street led down to the Marne" (*D*, 382). When he goes to her home, here is how he finds his way: "I followed the Marne" (*D*, 347), and one walk among many, taken alongside the river: "Around five, we went for a walk alongside the river" (*D*, 385). Even when the narrator imagines a hypothetical death-scene for his mistress, the river is part of it: "She would go to the edge of the Marne, catch cold, then die" (*D*, 434). There are many more examples. It is surely more than a coincidence, moreover, that the very consonance of the heroine's name—Marthe—is as close as a name can be to that of the river Marne and that both are close indeed to the word "mater" or "maternal." Each is, in its way, an archetypal, maternal, soothing presence.

In combination with the identification of place, Radiguet's very specific naming of dates and hours and moments makes for a very convincing narrative. These are never obtrusive. Nonetheless, dates and numbers are presented with quite astonishing frequency throughout *Devil in the Flesh,* giving it a most impressive specificity. Again and again, we are reminded of the day, the month, the year, or the time of day. We are told the age of the narrator, or that of Marthe. But Radiguet is extremely clever in the way in which he presents this information. It is never allowed to dominate the narrative, so that the story might turn into a report or a chronicle. Instead, it emerges inconspicuously. For example, the narrator describes the events leading up to his first making love with Marthe. He compares himself and her to Daphnis and Chloé. He slips in some quite detailed information by way of describing a dressing-gown that she offers him, as a form of invitation to make love to her: "On the day of my sixteenth birthday, in the month of March 1918, begging me not to get angry, Marthe made me a present of a dressing-gown resembling her own, which she wanted to see me wear when I was with her" (*D*, 344).

It is of course possible to set Radiguet's own life and the events of *Devil in the Flesh* side by side, in order to see to what extent the latter follows the former. In fact with the major exception of the conclusion, where Marthe dies in the novel, but Radiguet's mistress did not in the "real world," the two follow largely parallel paths. Certainly Radiguet is disingenuous in alleging that *Devil in the Flesh*, avoiding the mood of "anxiety," which was so fashionable in this period, also should not be seen as an autobiography or confession:

Will the reader be astonished to find in a book about adolescence none of that famous "anxiety" so in fashion in the last few years? But for the hero of *Devil in the Flesh* (who should not be confused with the author, notwithstanding the use of "I"), the interest is elsewhere. This interest arises more from the circumstances than from the hero himself. In the book, you see the freedom and idleness brought on by the war forming a young boy and killing a young woman. This little love-novel is not a confession, least of all when it most appears to be one. It is an all too human failing to believe only in the sincerity of someone who accuses himself; so, since the novel demands contrasts rarely to be found in life, it is natural that what is in fact a false autobiography should seem most true. [18]

Most of the novel is, in point of fact, autobiographical. Ultimately, however, it is the quality of Radiguet's writing, and not just the quality of his experience, that has allowed the work to survive. It is as experience transformed and shaped into a self-sufficient, aesthetically satisfying narrative that *Devil in the Flesh* must be examined. It is in the context of literature, rather than that of life or raw experience that its most important qualities emerge.

In order to understand the fictional point of view given in the novel, one must listen carefully to its very first lines: "I am going to leave myself open to many reproaches. Yet what can I do about it? Is it my fault if I had my twelfth birthday a few months before the declaration of war" (*D*, 289). From the very beginning, the narrator makes it perfectly clear that his point of view will be that of a child, not an adult. Consequently, the war will mean something quite different for him from what it does for a grown-up person. One must then ask oneself just what the war did mean for him. It is described as "this extraordinary period" and as a "four-year summer holiday" (*D*, 289). Whereas for most people war is the most unavoidable and drastic reality, bringing death and suffering in its wake, it is, for the narrator, something totally different. It is, on the contrary, a removal of and from customary reality. It is a set of extraordinary circumstances rendering possible events that otherwise could not take place. To be sure the war as war does enter the picture: "We could hear the cannon. There was fighting close to Meaux. People were even saying that some Uhlans had been captured near Lagny, fifteen kilometres from home" (D, 304). There are a number of such descriptions. But war in this novel is important not as history, pressing down with all its weight upon the lives of the protagonists. On the contrary, it frees the narrator from normal constraints, liberates him into a world where his scope for action is greater than in time of peace, and is the agent by which the weight of real life and responsibility is removed from his shoulders. It causes the barriers to come tumbling down. The narrator compares himself to a cat, attentively watching a piece of cheese under a glass dome. In effect, the war broke the glass dome: "I never have been a dreamer. What seems dreamlike to others more credulous than myself struck me as being as real as is the cheese for the cat, in spite of that glass dome. And yet the dome does exist. With the breaking of the dome, the cat seizes the opportunity, even if it is the masters who break it and cut their hands on it" (D, 290). In other words this is the story not of "the masters who cut their hands"—the adults engaged in war—but of the cat and the forbidden cheese: the child given the opportunity to do something that is normally unattainable.

When times are extraordinary, as they are here, it becomes perfectly normal for extraordinary occurrences to take place. We know that these extraordinary happenings will be possible only for as long as the war lasts. They begin with it, and end with its conclusion. The time it covers is not that of normal experience for the boy— it abstracts him from normal reality—instead, time is perceived as a series of moments of heightened perception and deepened significance. The first such moment suggests the uncanniness, strangeness, and ultimate impermanence of the world the narrator is about to enter. For adults, the imminence of war is suggested by the Caillaux affair (Caillaux was accused of corresponding with the enemy) and the assassination of Archduke Franz Ferdinand in Sarajevo. But the narrator's perception is neither political or historic: it is, rather, personal. Standing on the threshold of a new life, separating a prosaic past from a poetic future, is a suicide he witnessed. On the eve of July 14, 1914, a neighbor's maid climbed on the roof of her employer's house. While the latter, a town councilor named Maréchaud, overcome by the ignominy of the situation, hid in his house, the maid hurled imprecations at the crowd below, which was torn between the temptation of the nearby fair and the spectacle of the maid on the roof. She remained there from two o'clock in the afternoon until late in the evening, defying all the efforts of the firemen to rescue her. Finally, quite insane but somehow satisfied by the performance she had given, she plunged to her death, before the horrified gaze of the narrator, looking on with his father. The boy fainted and was taken to the edge of the Marne to recover.

The incident of the maid's death is significant for a number of reasons. There is, in the first place, the intrusion of the extraordinary into the banal life of a quiet town. Throughout Radiguet's critical essays, there is a sense of the need to endow recent events with a character of mythology, and indeed to search out supernal reality in apparently trite circumstances. This suicide is just an example of what Radiguet would call a mythical event, Joyce an epiphany, and Baudelaire a solemnity. Its profound significance might be hard to elucidate, but it is nonetheless real. In the words of the narrator: "If I insist upon such an episode, it is because it sheds light better than any other on that strange period of war, and shows how, more than the picturesque features of things, it was their poetry that impressed me" (D, 303). The maid, moreover, in uttering her incomprehensible words, is Cassandra-like, a figure of prophecy of dire events, whom nobody understands. Her very death, after a day of what might be called "entertainment," as she performed on the roof, is a "paradigm" for the narrator's perception of the war: four years of holidays, followed by a death—that of Marthe. Moreover this episode appears particularly appropriate as a model for many of the relationships presented in the novel. With the disappearance of paternal authority during the war, the men are at the front or, like the narrator's father, less strict than they would normally be, because of the circumstances: a world of freedom, but disorder and confusion are also allowed to develop. Maréchaud hides while his housemaid "performs" and then dies. Witchlike, she has prophesied a period of anarchy, a troubled time; like the witches of *Macbeth* announcing the start of an extraordinary period: "The charm's wound up,"[19] the maid sets the stage, prepares the reader for the unusual.

As though to enhance the extraordinary, uncanny, or mythical attributes of the incident involving Maréchaud and his maid, he is made into a grotesque figure, at home in a romance or a fairy tale. He is described as "a grotesque little man, a dwarf with a white goatee, wearing a hood" (*D, 297*). He is toadlike. And yet, as the elected officer of his fellow citizens, he represents and symbolizes his society. In fact, the relationship of the narrator to most figures of authority in this novel is an adversary relationship. We are confronted here, in a story ostensibly about life in the Marne in the course of World War I, with many echoes of traditional romance, going back to the tale of Tristan and Iseult. With the incident involving the suicide, *Devil in the Flesh* ceases to be simply a "confession" about a specific set of events in the Marne and becomes more than that; it is simultaneously a contemporary romance, whose time-frame is partly "July 14, 1914," etc., but also the "once upon a time" of a fairy tale or the *in ille tempore* of myth or legend.

The narrator makes no attempt to present time as an even flow; for him, it is not perceived as such. He may dwell on occasion for a good number of pages on a brief moment. On the other hand, time unredeemed by extraordinary circumstances is presented in a brief, schematic notation: "So three years went by with no other friendship and no other aspiration than our Thursday parties—with the little girls that my friend's parents provided us with in all innocence, inviting for snacks both the boys friendly with their son and the girls friendly with their daughter—small favors that we purloined from them, and they from us, under the cover of forfeits" (*D, 307*). In contrast to this "profane" or ordinary, dull time, the rhythm of the months and seasons associated with the growth of the narrator's friendship and love for Marthe has a different, more special quality. Months and seasons mark the progress of the love affair, and underline it.

Analysis: "Medieval" Attributes: Romance

Marthe and the narrator first meet in the month of April, in 1917. Spring is of course the traditional season for the birth of love. Superficially, the scene appears perfectly "realistic." They meet one Sunday. The narrator's father had organized a walk in the company of the Grangier family: Marthe, her sickly younger brother, and their parents. Without transgressing natural law, without stretching our credulity, and in a perfectly straightforward fashion, Radiguet presents a scene that is edenic in its loveliness. Its paradisiac character is suggested by the setting; they walk alongside a narrow stream to Ormesson. They cross meadows strewn with wild flowers, while the river carries down thousands of pink and white petals from hawthorn trees. The impression of a garden, of nature brought under control and made beautiful and bountiful, is perpetuated and reinforced by the presence at their feet of clumps of watercress and mint.

The walk with Marthe is a form of revelation for the narrator. His first glimpse of her could readily be compared to a sort of epiphany, notwithstanding the casual and even banal vocabulary used by Radiguet to describe her appearance. The narrator's family meets up with the Grangier family in the train station of La Varenne. The narrator is dismayed by what he sees. Her family is unattractive and he imagines that she, who is to arrive shortly, having missed the train, will likewise be plain and dull. In fact, when her train enters the station, she is standing on the running-board, dressed simply, in contrast to the frumpy, contrived fussiness of her mother. The narrator is immediately captivated: "The reckless girl entranced me" (D, 310).

Since the Middle Ages, it has been characteristic of romantic love that it should derive from sudden illumination. As the affair between Marthe and the narrator develops, it fulfills the other typical conditions of love as it appears in the medieval love romances. Like many another lady of the Middle Ages, Marthe is left alone by her husband, who has gone off to war, and the lover who takes his place is not distinguished for his martial qualities. What is more, Marthe is remarkable, after her initial emergence in a gesture of defiance, for being defined only, wholly, and absolutely by her love. Indeed, outside the love that ennobles her, she scarcely exists! We have no idea of what she looks like or how she spends her time. Measured objectively, by the standards of life, rather than by the quality of her love, she is a drab, dull personage, of rather limited intelligence, with mediocre artistic talent and even poor taste in house-furnishings! Whereas her fiancé is fond of interior decoration in the style of Louis XV, her own bad taste runs to Japanese things (D, 323).

The words Henry James used to describe the characteristics of the romance might equally be applied to *Devil in the Flesh*. We are brought face to face with experience "liberated . . . experience disengaged, disembroiled, disencumbered, exempt from the conditions that we normally know to attach to it."[20] The love affair takes place, to be sure, during the war, surrounded by the "real" world. But in fact it inhabits a private, separate "world." The love is private and must be kept secret, and takes place largely at night. It advances in a series of stages and initiations; it is governed by rites and marked by signs.[21] The love is intensified by difficulty and frustration, and it lifts the lovers to a new plane of being. On the one hand, Radiguet is unusually specific in naming times and dates and places; but on the other, with the growth of the love between Marthe and the narrator, there is a blurring effect, a quality of mystery that is imparted to time, space, and circumstance. Increasingly, objects and places assume importance as signifiers of love, rather than as referents to "real life."

The immediate effect of the narrator's meeting Marthe is to create a distance between him and his friend of three years' standing, René. This first contact with Marthe, and indeed the whole of *Devil in the Flesh,* may be considered to form a sentimental education, the story of the passage from childhood into adult life. At the same time that his love for Marthe grows, and that for René diminishes, so too his relationship to his family becomes more distant. Thanks to a chance encounter with Marthe on the way to Paris, he spends the day with her, dictates the choice of furniture for the house she will share with her husband during the latter's leaves, and opens the possibility of renewed acquaintance with her.

About one month after Marthe's marriage to Jacques, contracted during one of his leaves, she writes to the narrator, to invite him to visit her in her home in J. . . . From this moment on, he will enter a world that strikes us as strangely private, nocturnal, secret, enclosed, and feminine. It is a world of the inside, and in its very isolation it creates a sense that everything taking place there is intensified.

The street on which Marthe lives leads down to the river Marne. Her house is not of course a castle, but it does impress the narrator with its size. Moreover, like the heroine of a medieval romance living in a tower, she lives on the top floor. The apartment is not literally difficult to attain, but he does have difficulty. He is filled with apprehension. Marthe has lit a fire, and the leaping flames make him believe that a fire has broken out! He cannot find the doorbell; then, having received directions from the landlady, identified simply as *une vieille femme* ("an old woman") downstairs, he stumbles up to the apartment (*D,* 332).

On the night the two first make love, reaching Marthe's place is an ordeal for the youth. He has led his mother to believe that he would leave the family home early in the morning in order to go on a picnic with René. In fact, he slips out late the night before, with his picnic basket, carefully prepared by his mother. This is one of a number of tribulations or humiliations that, like an ironic Lancelot, he must undergo so as to be united with Marthe. He hides his hamper, after some hesitation, making of his action a life-or-death venture: "I hesitated for a long time, paler than a man setting a dynamite fuse. But I did indeed hide the provisions" (*D,* 348). By this time, Marthe has provided him not with a ring, in the medieval courtly tradition, but, more practically, with a key to her apartment. In a Freudian situation too obvious to need commentary,[22] he cannot at first find the keyhole. Then, when he enters the vestibule, he stumbles against the umbrella stand, is afraid of pressing the wrong switch, thereby activating the bell instead of the light, and almost wishes to turn tail and run. In a modern, ironic mode, this is reminiscent of the trials and humiliations the traditional, would-be lover has had to overcome in order to make his way to the inaccessible tower, where the lady has been locked up for safe keeping by her husband.

Analysis: "Medieval" Attributes: The *Alba*

The most beautiful scenes of the novel are no doubt those which take place within Marthe's apartment, where the two lovers are united. Here, the relationship of occupant to abode is mysterious and fascinating, almost magic. This becomes a special space. And the links connecting Radiguet's narrative to medieval conventions are strengthened and sharpened.

Frequently, the action of a medieval erotic poem will take place in an intimate space, a secluded alcove or chamber. Whereas at first the knight may be content with the mere contemplation of the other's body, or a furtive kiss, soon this will no longer suffice, and he will become obsessed with the desire to see her undress, to find and observe her asleep, or the desire actually to leave a mark on her, and to embrace her naked body. In the words of Bernard de Ventadour: "And I would kiss her mouth in all directions, so much

so that for one whole month the mark would be seen there."[23]
Beyond such compulsions, the eventual, ultimate refinement of bliss
is of course consummation: the mingling of the two naked bodies.

Similary, the narrator in *Devil in the Flesh* advances by stages.
First he is satisfied to look upon Marthe. Then, he and she kiss.
Later, he is agitated by the obsessive desire to "leave his mark" on
her: "In my ecstasy I bit her skin where it was exposed, so that her
mother would suspect her of having a lover. I would have liked to
be able to leave my initials there. My childish savagery rediscovered
the ancient meaning of tattoos. Marthe kept on saying: "Yes, bite
me, mark me, I want everybody to know" (*D*, 340–41).

Marthe's apartment becomes an extraordinary, intimate place for
the lovers. The beauty of nature is brought indoors, as an olive-
wood fire spreads its fragrance through the room. The hangings and
carpets, soft to the touch, like animal skins, make the small space
even more intimate. Marthe, illumined by the firelight, is never
more beautiful than in this setting. The fire itself divides space into
two separate zones. In the first, bathed in its light, Marthe and the
boy embrace. The second is an outer ring of darkness. "If one moved
away from it [the fire] it was dark, and one bumped into the table
and chairs" (*D*, 333–34).

On the actual night of love-making, this room is transformed
into a mysterious place of initiation, as the boy, having left his
mother's picnic basket outside, is undressed by Marthe, since he
has been soaked by the rain, before they make love. This room loses
its "profane" or ordinary character and becomes a more meaningful,
extraordinary, and significant area, comparable, for example, to the
Minnegrotte as it is described in Gottfried von Strassburg's *Tristan
and Isolde*. As in that work, food seems to be a prosaic reminder of
the world outside the Minnegrotte, the cave of love. Marthe's room
is separated from society and the world at large. In Gottfried's
Tristan, the separation is visibly radical in terms of space and time.
The lovers must cross barren land for two days before reaching their
cave, and there is a huge wild forest at the foot of the mountain in
which the cave is hollowed out:

> But all around and down the slope
> Stood trees without number . . .
> From this mountain and this cave
> For a full day's journey

> Stretched rocks with no fields
> And wasteland and wilderness
> There was no opportunity
> Of getting to it by roads or paths. [24]

Just as this space is qualitatively different from the space around it, so too time is different in quality. The room seems to recede into a primitive or mythical past. This too was one of the attributes of Gottfried's *Minnegrotte* in his *Tristan:*

> That same cave had been hewn
> Into the wild mountain
> At the time of the pagans
> Before the reign of Corineis
> When giants ruled
> There within they had their hiding place
> When they wished to be by themselves
> And make love. [25]

The medieval coloring of the work is further enhanced; the scene appears very reminiscent of the traditional situation presented in the medieval *alba,* or erotic poem of dawn, in which two lovers join inside the lady's chamber, and are interrupted in the morning—or indeed separated—by the rising sun, the call of the birds, or the voice of the castle watchman.

The morning after their first night of love-making, the couple in *Devil in the Flesh* are awoken by the sound of Marthe's mother, knocking at the door. Puzzled at getting no response, the mother leaves. On another occasion, the narrator encounters the milkman first thing in the morning, at the door. The milkman immediately comprehends what is going on. On still another occasion, Marthe's neighbors invite in friends to listen to the couple's love-making. They are foiled in this attempt. But all of these incidents suggest the typical world of the *alba,* in which the lovers on the inside, in a kind of closed paradise, a *paradisus claustralis,* are confronted, surrounded, beset, and eventually defeated by the world of the outside: the gossipers (or *losengiers* of the medieval poem), the pillars of respectability, the representatives of society and morality.

Just as the second act of Wagner's *Tristan und Isolde* may be viewed as a greatly expanded *alba,* so too it is possible to see in *Devil in the Flesh* or at least the major part, which presents the love affair between the narrator and Marthe, the strategy of the *alba*. Their love is illicit and unacceptable in the eyes of society. There is a dichotomy between their life and love and the life of "others." Their life is largely nocturnal, and led on the "inside." Increasingly, the outside world encroaches upon them, as was inevitable. Marthe's mother raises questions, as does the narrator's. The milkman spreads the word about the affair. The downstairs neighbors, thwarted in their attempt to have their friends hear the couple's love-making, are filled with hatred for the two. Marthe's landlords refuse to speak to her. In the narrator's words, "This was when J . . . opened fire on her" (*D,* 378). This is not of course literally true. Marthe and the narrator are not divided by the family enmity of the Capulets pitted against the Montagues. Nor does the course of their love run as deep and straight as that of Romeo and Juliet. Nonetheless it becomes clear that their love must end in separation and misfortune, as surely as day follows night.

The minor encroachments upon their love are only an attenuated prefiguration of the final, great dawn: the Armistice, which involves the awakening to reality, the reintroduction of normal life, an end put to the extraordinary circumstances—the kind of night—that made this liaison possible. The return of peace is the final episode in a pattern of events involving a curious reversal of values. The return of law and peace and order is for the narrator a time of separation, of alienation, and of death. Marthe's death in childbirth coincides with the termination of hostilities. This pattern of reversal is characteristic both of the *alba* and of *Devil in the Flesh.* In each, the act of love is, or is seen as, an act of aggression against society and its fundamental social contract, marriage. This adulterous love may be—in fact is—beautiful, but it is illicit and makes no claim to being anything else. In *Devil in the Flesh,* as in the *alba,* loyalty, patriotism, heroism, skill, and strength are not the attributes of the young lover, but belong rather in the outside world. Jacques, Marthe's husband, remains rather two-dimensional; but just about everything we learn about him reveals him in a positive light. The narrator, on the other hand, lacks loyalty, fidelity, and constancy in his love. He tries to make love to Svea, a friend of Marthe's. His perversity is such that he is unkind toward Marthe and jealous of her husband just as soon as he realizes how important physical relations can be. Communication between them is by no means harmonious, and this is largely his fault, because of his excessively critical attitude. He is, to a considerable degree, responsible for his mistress's death.

The events going from the narrator's first encounter with Marthe until her death and the conclusion of the story follow an appropriately seasonal movement. They first make love in the spring of 1918. In the summer, they are able to spend some time together in Marthe's parents' house—the latter are of course absent—in an idyllic interlude. The narrator here busies himself tending the garden and pulling out weeds. It must have been about this time that their baby was conceived, and the tending of the garden is an obvious suggestion of fertility. They leave this house in September, at which moment the narrator immediately understands that his happiness is about to desert him. This season of decline is an apt counterpoint to the imminent end of the life and love they share.

The narrator's relationship to Marthe is by no means a constant sharing of love, interrupted only by the Armistice and Marthe's death. On the one hand is Marthe, who does come to owe all of her interest and existence to love itself; she is quite devoted and even subservient in her feelings, and the reader rapidly reaches the conclusion that, deprived of this love, she must of necessity die. Love is her character, her body, her spirit, and meaning in life. Facing her is the narrator, caught in a constantly fluctuating movement, an oscillation between love and exasperation. Cruelty, the cruelty of the child, is very much present in him. He possesses a form of cruel devilment, malicious teasing, and an impatient restlessness all suggested in the title of the novel, alongside genuine love. He is in truth responsible for the circumstances that cause Marthe to fall sick and die.

On one occasion, the narrator's perverseness leads him to insist that Marthe, now pregnant, should spend the night with him. It is winter, and to satisfy his whim she is obliged to accompany him to the cold and dirt of Paris. He lacks the courage, in view of his age, and out of ashamed embarrassment that Marthe is visibly pregnant, to speak to a hotel clerk and take a room for the two of them. After this wretched incident, she goes home in the train in his company, exhausted and unhappy. She falls sick and, sometime later, in the month of January, dies in giving birth to their son, who is two months premature. This baby is assumed by the husband, Jacques, but presumably by nobody else, to be his own. The husband's convenient naiveté allows for rather a tidy conclusion. On the last page, the narrator describes his perception of a reestablished order, of restored harmony. The narrator understands that, in the final analysis, order does take over, and that his son "would have a reasonable existence" (*D,* 457).

Analysis: The Conclusion

The conclusion, which apparently was suggested by Cocteau, is not perhaps as satisfactory as it first appears. In the first place, there is an intrinsic lack of suspense in the lovers' situation and in the conclusion toward which the narrative inexorably moves. One can understand that it was only with the help—and thanks to the vigorous prompting—of Jean Cocteau that Radiguet was able to write a conclusion. The narrative strategy, in running parallel to that of the *alba,* gains in the dramatic tension it creates between the lovers on the one hand and society on the other. But it loses also, insofar as the reader is soon aware that the outcome or resolution must entail the triumph of society over the couple as surely as dawn follows darkness. And Radiguet's conclusion—Marthe's death in childbirth, Jacques's return and acceptance of the child as his own, and the end of the war—seems too contrived to be entirely plausible. Finally, notwithstanding the narrator's claim that harmony is restored, the reader, on the contrary, does not have the impression of justice done or balance reestablished. There remains a lingering distaste for the narrator; surely, in any restoration of order, he should have been punished at least as much as Marthe. After all, Iseult did not die alone, any more than did Juliet! At the end of *Romeo and Juliet,* the public must perforce agree with the Prince of Verona's insistence upon the general sadness of the story that has just been presented; dawn, here, brings sadness, grief over the death of the two young lovers:

> A glooming peace this morning with it brings,
> The sun for sorrow will not show his head.
> Go hence, to have more talk of these sad things.
> Some shall be pardoned and some punished.
> For never was a story of more woe
> Than this Juliet and her Romeo.[26]

In Shakespeare's play, suffering and death are shared equally. On the other hand, *Devil in the Flesh* leaves the impression of a pattern left incomplete, not quite satisfactory. In fairness to Radiguet, one must add that *Devil in the Flesh* is written in the first-person singular, and there is simply no plausible way that the narrator could have recounted his experience from beyond the grave. He had to be kept alive!

Analysis: Radiguet's Achievement and Debt

With *Devil in the Flesh,* Raymond Radiguet achieved a prodigious tour de force, a novel that is on the whole very successful at a time when novels were considered to be discredited. At the age of seventeen, he proved that the novel could still capture all the subtleties of a complex psychology in the twentieth century. Still more remarkable is the fact that, drawing upon the raw experience of his own life, he created a coherent work of art having much in common with medieval literary forms. To be sure, he must have examined other models with great care. One thinks in particular of Laclos's *Les Liaisons Dangereuses,* Fromentin's *Dominique,* and more particularly Benjamin Constant's *Adolphe;* the latter was reprinted twice in 1920, more than a hundred years after it first appeared, and appears to have been known to Radiguet. Certainly Radiguet seems to have profited from a close reading of the epistolary novel *Les Liaisons Dangereuses,* or of novels in which letters play an important part, such as *Adolphe.* Letters are used to extremely good effect in *Devil in the Flesh.* They are in no way obtrusive; but they are present throughout the narrative. A letter announces the marriage of Jacques and Marthe to the narrator. One month later, it is in a letter that Marthe urges him to come to see her and complains about his neglect of her. Jacques writes to Marthe every day, and she tosses these letters into the fire, as she lies alongside the narrator. When Jacques writes disconsolately to say how easy it would be to die, it is the narrator who dictates to Marthe the tender letter she sends in reply! When Marthe's parents perceive that the narrator is writing to her, they burn his letters before her very eyes! And it is with a joyful letter that Marthe announces the birth of their son.

The letters in *Devil in the Flesh* serve several useful functions. In the first place, Jacques's frequent letters serve as a counterpoise to the love affair between the narrator and Marthe. Whereas they live in the present, his letters are a constant reminder that the past and the future do exist, that there is an outside world that must inevitably encroach upon them. In burning his letters, Marthe in effect banishes concerns other than her present love. But the narrator's unease or disquiet remains. He cannot forget that Jacques was there before him, and will no doubt be there again. They do indeed bring to life the possibility of this threat, with Jacques's writing to indicate that he will be brought back wounded from the front, and will be passing through the town of J. . . .

In addition, the letters in this novel underline a rather basic pessimism regarding human communication. At the beginning of their love affair, Marthe writes letters that are admirable; the text of these is not given at all. At this point a perfect harmony or symmetry is suggested in the relationship. In most cases, however, the letters reveal flawed communication of one sort or another. In almost every case, the letters bring out a fundamental asymmetry or disparity or distance between the writer and the recipient or addressee. Jacques sends tender letters that are burned. Those he receives are dictated by his wife's lover. When Marthe lies dying, the narrator begins an angry letter of insult that becomes a letter of apology. His letters are burned by Marthe's parents. Earlier, Marthe had justly accused him of betraying her with her friend Svea. But the narrator writes a deceitful letter that convinces Marthe her fears are unfounded, and this induces her to write to her landlady to announce that the narrator should be allowed to visit her apartment with anyone he wishes. The love shared by Marthe and the narrator briefly lifts them to a plane of existence where there is no need for formal communication, verbal or written. But, when letters are written, they more often than not involve deceit, misunderstanding, or disappointment.

From a strictly technical, narrative point of view, the letters do seem useful and even necessary. The danger of monotony in *Devil in the Flesh* is real but never realized. The point of view of the first-person narrator is of necessity limited. In effect, in beginning the affair with Marthe, he withdraws into a small world: a tiny cast of characters, a small stage, one main preoccupation, love. Thanks to the letters, other characters are brought into the action: Jacques especially, but also the parents of both protagonists, and the larger outside world are brought into focus and made to seem real.

The borrowings in *Devil in the Flesh* are relatively minor and the originality of the work is considerable. Radiguet denied himself the use of picturesque detail to hold the reader's attention; for example, we know nothing about the lovers' appearance, nothing about what becomes of the youth after his affair, not even his name! Nonetheless, he is complex: perverse and naive, he is endowed with life thanks to Radiguet's art. Similarly, we scarcely see Jacques Lacombe, except through Marthe, who is herself a shadowy or evanescent figure, or through the letters they exchange. But he too is brought to life by the author. Finally, even the Marne, as river and region, is a real presence, and almost a "character" in *Devil in the Flesh:* both poetic and true to life, a suitable setting and an appropriate complement.

Chapter Four
Count d'Orgel

Upon receiving a copy of *Devil in the Flesh,* the poet Paul Valéry wrote to thank the author and, having complimented him upon his talent, advised him to remain outside literary fads and fashions, free of the temptation to keep on repeating himself: "It is difficult to pay you compliments which differ from the things that are being printed. So I shall limit my remarks to the wish that you will preserve complete freedom of mind. It is of the utmost importance. In respect to your first book, keep the same independence that it displays . . . with regard to what was in vogue when you were writing it."[1] Although *Le Bal du comte d'Orgel* (translated as *Ball at Count d'Orgel's,* then, more simply, as *Count d'Orgel*),[2] Radiguet's second novel (1924), also tells the story of the burgeoning of an adulterous love affair, it is in fact quite different from the first, and indeed from any other novel of the time. Radiguet did indeed "preserve complete freedom of mind."

Written in the third person, not the first, *Count d'Orgel* takes place in the postwar Parisian world in 1920, presenting the essentially aristocratic company that is grouped around the Count d'Orgel and his wife, Mahaut, who is of a very distinguished noble house, the Grimoard de la Verberie. Having left France in the seventeenth century for Martinique, her family had come back at the turn of the twentieth, in 1902. Whereas the love affair in *Devil in the Flesh* completed a cycle that included the death and the birth of a child, that which is described in *Count d'Orgel* remains unconsummated, potential, virtual, and platonic. Radiguet may well have been following here the pattern established by the seventeenth-century novel *The Princess of Cleves,* by Mme de Lafayette, which was said to be a model for him. Be that as it may, the young François de Séryeuse, who is of noble origin also, falls in love with Mahaut and she with him. Toward the end of the work, each learns indirectly that this love is returned, but the actual ending of the story offers neither solution nor resolution. The Count d'Orgel, a somewhat fatuous figure as a rule, summons up authority when he learns of the love shared by François and Mahaut. He does not try to dismiss the man. Instead, he insists that François should still be among the guests at the count's forthcoming fancy dress ball, the "Ball" of the French title, and that the embarrassing situation must be patched over. The final words of the novel are his, to his wife: "And now, Mahaut, sleep. This I command" (*B*, 194). One can only speculate about further relations among the three, but it seems clear that they will be unhappy. There is no sense of that restoration of order or of an "orderly existence"[3] to be found at the end of *Devil in the Flesh*.

Circumstances of Composition

Count d'Orgel was largely written in the summer and fall of 1922, but was not published until July 1924, some seven months after Radiguet's death. The summer of 1922 was particularly productive for both Cocteau and Radiguet. First at the Grand Hotel in the Lavandou and then at the Villa "Croix Fleurie" Cocteau worked on his novels *Le Grand Ecart* (The splits) and *Thomas l'imposteur* (Thomas, the impostor) as well as his long love-poem *Plain-Chant* (Plainsong) and a modern version of the play *Antigone*.[4] Radiguet, his constant companion, revised *Devil in the Flesh,* then composed the first draft of *Count d'Orgel*. The presence, for a time, of Georges Auric, François de Gouy d'Arcy, and the American Russell Greeley did not distract the two from their efforts. Then, with the departure of the others, Cocteau and Radiguet worked on in silence. From the beginning, Cocteau sensed that his companion was in the throes of writing a work of great importance. Cocteau's correspondence gives a clear idea of his astonished, if exaggerated, response to Radiguet's efforts. In July 1922 he describes the first pages of *Count d'Orgel* as "lovelier than Proust and truer than Balzac." His enthusiasm continued unabated as the work progressed, for he described it, in the following months, as "a prodigious thing," "an incredible thing," "indisputably one of the finest novels that exist," and believed that it put to shame even Stendhal and Balzac![5]

Cocteau was not content merely to applaud from the wings. His generous praise was accompanied by freely given advice and even much more. In the first place, Cocteau assumed the role of taskmaster to his pupil. The initial manuscript, for example, was about four hundred pages long. Cocteau, with help from Georges Auric, obliged Radiguet to shorten the work considerably. When Radiquet finished his first draft, moreover, Cocteau made it clear that this was only a beginning: "Radiguet finished his book yesterday. This means that he is starting it again—for he must put it in order as he copies." And he adds: "I gave him the concluding word."[6] This suggestion of an active contribution by Cocteau to *Count d'Orgel* has been abundantly confirmed. To some extent, the two writers wished to avoid a repetition of the criticism that assailed *Devil in the Flesh* when it appeared; its numerous spelling and grammatical errors had been pointed out by the critics. But Cocteau's modifications were not limited to work on solecisms. In addition, he made major revisions, affecting, for example, both the beginning and the end. Radiguet, in his lifetime, conceded his friend's assistance: "This morning, I began to redo the beginning of *Count d'Orgel* poorly balanced—Jean helped me."[7]

On his return to Paris in November 1922 Radiguet was too preoccupied by the impending publication of *Devil in the Flesh,* as well as by an unusually active social life, to continue revising his second novel. Only in the summer of the following year were the revisions resumed. In October 1923 the manuscript was given to Grasset. That, one might suppose, was the end of it. Cocteau certainly claimed that Radiguet, having written the work, then assumed responsibility for seeing to the page-proofs immediately before his death: "This *Ball,* he would receive the proofs for it, in the hotel room where fever consumed him. He took it upon himself to make no alterations."[8] This version of events was essentially confirmed by the writer Joseph Kessel, who was then a proofreader with Grasset. When the book did appear, it was hailed by a critic as being "very good Cocteau,"[9] but the defunct author's friends, led by Cocteau himself, ridiculed this notion and succeeded in quelling it. It was only fifty years later that a comparison of the proofs with the published *Count d'Orgel* as it has come down to us revealed that the latter differs in many places from the former. There appears to have been a benign conspiracy involving Grasset, Cocteau, and Kessel to conceal the changes made to Radiguet's manuscript after his death with a view to improving it. Many tenses were changed, words that appeared inelegant were replaced, unclear expressions were rendered differently, and blank spaces were introduced between episodes, providing, in effect, unnumbered chapter divisions. In sum, *Count d'Orgel* as we know it is primarily Radiguet's creation; but Cocteau's part in its shaping is of great importance.

Once more, Cocteau had displayed his ungovernable talents as stage manager, director, or impresario; he not only guided Radiguet and held him to the task of composition, but also went so far as to "correct" the manuscript before and after the younger man's death, and, when the book appeared, tried to secure the best reviews possible. And he nipped in the bud any notion that *Count d'Orgel* was not the creation of Raymond Radiguet, working by himself. It was an astonishing performance. Cocteau's motives can scarcely be impugned; he wished to obtain, in the publication of the second novel, a kind of literary epiphany, a consecration of his charge, an event of perfection. Nonetheless his intervention must be seen as regrettable.

Analysis of the Action

Like *Devil in the Flesh, Count d'Orgel* begins with an adroit prolepsis: that is to say, an anticipation of possible objections. The narrator forestalls and parries a possible claim by the reader that the Countess d'Orgel may appear implausible. This opening is positively brilliant in its summing up of some of the novel's major themes:

Are the movements of a heart like that of the Countess d'Orgel obsolete? Such a blend of duty and supineness will perhaps seem incredible in our day, even in a person of noble strain who is Creole. Is it perhaps the case that we are not attracted to purity on the grounds that it is less delectable than disorder?

But the unconscious workings of a pure soul are still stranger than the machinations of vice. That is what we reply to those women who on the one hand will find Mme d'Orgel too honorable and, on the other, too promiscuous. (*B,* 17)

Count d'Orgel is indeed the examination, long before Nathalie Sarraute's *Tropisms,* of the interior workings and movements of the heart: here fallen victim to love and temptation. Heart, race, purity, order, and disorder are all terms of central importance in the novel. The work is a tour de force insofar as it sustains the reader's interest without using the traditional devices of the modern novel; the subject matter is minimal, the description of material realities is very slight, the incidents that occur are, viewed objectively, trivial, and there are few surprises and no life-or-death-dealing episodes.

While the actual action presented in *Count d'Orgel* takes place over an eight-month period in 1920, the temporal "reach" or significant time frame of the work is much greater. In sequence, the novel proceeds as follows. Mahaut d'Orgel is presented as the scion of an old French noble family, which, offended by the encroachments of Louis XIII's royal power in the seventeenth century, had left France for Martinique. There, their noble haughtiness had mellowed under the effects of climate and financial success. With the passage of the centuries, the Grimoard de la Verberie family extends its influence throughout the island and remains an interested, if distant, observer of the historical events—and especially the Revolution— that sweep over France. They are not too critical of their relative Josephine, unhappy in love, married first to the Viscount de Beau-harnais and then to Napoleon. The family is forced to resume res-idence in France by the volcanic eruption of 1902, which devastated Saint-Pierre. Only after this long description and a briefer one of the Count d'Orgel, whom Mahaut marries at the age of eighteen (he is a young thirty), does the action proper begin. On Saturday, February 7, 1920, François de Séryeuse, a nonchalant but highly esteemed youth of twenty, goes to the Medrano Circus with his friend Paul Robin, a young diplomat who is excessively eager to succeed not only in his career but also in his social standing; at the circus, they both meet the Count and Countess d'Orgel.

For the rest of the novel, François's fate will be linked to that of this couple. Descriptions of the contacts between this group and their friends, and of the growing love between Mahaut and François, are interspersed with rather detailed information about the char-acters' family backgrounds; there is a paucity of information about Paul Robin and an overtly seductive American woman, Hester Wayne, who joins the band on some of their meetings. Hester Wayne and Paul Robin appear to be the only principal characters who are not of a "distinguished"—that is noble—family.

From the Medrano, that Saturday, the count and countess and their entourage, including François and Paul, Hester Wayne, and the Princess Hortense d'Austerlitz, go to the Robinson, a dancing establishment in the suburbs of Paris. At the Robinson, which is installed in a huge palace, they encounter Prince Mirza of Persia, a cousin to the shah; a widower, he is often accompanied by his fifteen-year-old niece, whose spouse is also dead. This first outing has about it some of the allure of an initiation for François, involving a night journey to a place of excitement, some hint of danger,[10] a

brush with a seductress, Hester Wayne, and the beginning of love
for a pure woman, taking place in a castle.

In the months that follow, adopting a seasonal rhythm, the love
between Mahaut and François grows, though they hardly dare admit
this to themselves, let alone to each other. François becomes a close
friend of both count and countess, is received frequently for lunch
by them, while his mother in turn, who is a widow, invites them
to lunch in her house in Champigny, in the Marne, near Paris.
Mme de Séryeuse, who is only thirty-seven, approves of her son's
new friends and even discovers that Mahaut and François are distant
cousins. For fear of overprotecting François, his mother had main-
tained a rather distant relationship with him; he lives most of the
time in Paris, not with her but with an old friend of the family,
Mme Forbach, who is blind and widowed—this latter condition is
a recurring pattern in the book—and has a retarded, hydrocephaloid
son.

In the summer, the affection between Mahaut and François grows
more intense; with the departure of their friends, they and the count
see much more of each other, and Mahaut perceives that François
shares her fondness for gardens and nature, which her husband does
not. A separation does take place, however, as François forces himself
to leave Paris, going on vacation to the Basque country, while shortly
afterwards the Orgels for their part head for Vienna.

When the three meet again in the autumn, in Paris, a crisis is
reached, as Mahaut becomes conscious of her love for François and
confesses this love in a long letter to his mother. The latter unwisely
lets Mahaut know that she in turn is loved, and makes the dilemma
still more acute by showing Mahaut's letter to her son. It is at this
point that a dinner at the count's is to take place, a preparatory
event at which to begin planning for a fancy-dress ball to open the
social season lavishly, in the month of October.

For fear of appearing discourteous toward his host, or perhaps
arousing his suspicions, François accepts the invitation to attend
the dinner over his mother's objections. Here, united in one room,
are all the count's "regulars," with, additionally, the Prince Naroumov, driven penniless from his home in Russia by the Bolshevik
Revolution, and newly arrived in Paris by way of Vienna. His
suffering and visible dejection cast a pall over the evening's frivolous
preparations for the masked ball, as does Mahaut's distress. Her
virtue and loyalty to her husband are strained by François's presence

and by the count's behavior; quite unwittingly, the latter mocks Naroumov by using his Tyrolean hat as a fancy-dress prop and executing the steps of a cossack dance. Out of a sense of devotion, Mahaut joins Anne in his indelicate behavior and turns some of the attention away from him. But the drain on her emotions is so great that she comes close to fainting.

In the final scene of the novel, in the couple's bedroom, Mahaut confesses her love and upbraids her spouse for his tactless comportment. She is distressed by his equanimity and inability to grasp the seriousness of their predicament. His solution, which is really not one, is the advice, at the very end, that Mahaut should sleep, and that they should carry on as though nothing had happened. Just as the opening of the novel reached into the past, implying that Mahaut's fortunes—and indeed those of almost all the characters— were shaped and conditioned by the patterns and vicissitudes of her ancestry, so the conclusion points to the future, and the reader is not bound by the mere eight months of the central events of the story. The ultimate conclusion is not provided by Radiguet: it is up to the reader to complete the design. The apparent inability to bring the work to full closure is reminiscent of Radiguet's ending in *Devil in the Flesh,* but also of the situation of Jacques Forestier, the principal protagonist in Jean Cocteau's *Le Grand Ecart,* at the end of that novel.[11]

Background

Radiguet's initiation into Parisian society appears to have been a major part of the background to *Count d'Orgel.* In the winter of 1919–20, Cocteau introduced him to the Count and Countess de Beaumont. It is clear that they served as principal models for Anne and Mahaut. Each year the Beaumonts held an extraordinarily lavish fancy-dress ball, a highlight of the Paris season. Artists who included Satie, Tzara, Cocteau, and Picasso were enlisted to help "design" it, while many actors and dancers would take part in the rehearsals for it. This ball may well have been in Radiguet's mind as the source for the one planned in his novel. Count Etienne de Beaumont, who was "of aquiline, aristocratic appearance . . . of exquisite manners, of taste, of flair and frivolity . . .,"[12] had much in common with his fictional counterpart, as this description indicates. He had displayed nerve and courage in World War I, as does Anne. While the Beaumonts were of fairly modest nobility, there was confusion, to their advantage, between their name and an older, more distinguished family, the Duke de Beaumont of the house of Montmorency; a similar misunderstanding benefits Anne in *Count d'Orgel*. In addition, while Etienne de Beaumont was devoted to his wife, Edith, he also had a fondness for artistic young men. In *Count d'Orgel*, there are hints of sexual ambivalence,[13] not the least of which is the count's name, Anne. In doing his research for his novel, Radiguet was undoubtedly aware that Anne, the Duke of Montmorency, is one of the characters entering into Mme de Lafayette's *The Princess of Cleves;* nonetheless, even to a French ear, the name has a distinctly feminine ring and causes the reader to think first of a woman.[14]

For each of the characters of the novel, it is not too difficult to draw a parallel with real-life counterparts from the period. Mahaut has much in common with Edith de Beaumont, most notably her sensitivity, seriousness, and even her voice; but other influences shaped the character, in particular that of Radiguet's own mother. François de Séryeuse appears to be an idealized alter ego of Radiguet himself, while Paul Robin appears to be a composite, drawing upon the novelist Paul Morand, who was in fact in the diplomatic corps, but also upon the composer Georges Auric, whose ambition and attraction to the aristocracy were well known.[15]

At the same time that Radiguet's acquaintances are a major source for *Count d'Orgel*, his readings very much shaped the form it took. Notwithstanding many superficial differences, there are significant similarities between it on the one hand and, on the other, Cocteau's *Thomas l'imposteur* and Alain-Fournier's *Le Grand Meaulnes.* In each of these three works, a young hero is initiated into a new, almost mythical world from which the pressures of mundane, everyday reality are removed.

Cocteau contended that Radiguet, in composing *Count d'Orgel,* "set up his easel" before Mme de Lafayette's *The Princess of Cleves* and used it as his model. Even a cursory examination of the two works bears him out. The description of illicit but chaste love involving, as major elements, a ball and a confession scene, and presenting a group of nobles living in a small world of decorum, elegance, and frequent boredom, from which material considerations are banished: these are just the most obvious of many similarities that reveal the influence of Mme de Lafayette on Radiguet. While the twentieth-century work does not offer the convenience of a retreat to a convent—Madame de Clèves's means of escaping from her love for the Duke de Nemours and the temptation he represents—Radiguet likewise offers no sign that the love between François and Mahaut will be consummated.

It is no exaggeration to say that *Count d'Orgel* was hailed as a landmark in the evolution of the psychological novel by a number of critics. Even Jacques Rivière, otherwise doubtful of Radiguet's lasting worth as a writer, admired this work's understated moderation in comparison to the entanglements more typical of the genre.[16] Thibaudet praised it highly, and was full of admiration for Radiguet's "abstract intelligence."[17] And André Gide, while stressing Radiguet's debt to Gobineau and regretting a number of stylistic lapses in the middle of the book, lavished praise on *Count d'Orgel:*

After *Le Grand Meaulnes,* read *Count d'Orgel,* which I did not know either. Extraordinary soundness of this book; almost too much. It partakes of the nature of a wager or an acrobatic feat. The result is virtually total success . . . Far superior to all of Radiguet's other productions, and to *Le Grand Meaulnes,* of which the interest is fading.[18]

A recurring theme of the critics is the work's soundess or sureness of touch. The reader does have the impression that the work is informed by a rather self-confident and convincing vision or aesthetic; in a word, it is a work of considerable maturity.

The lives presented by Radiguet in *Count d'Orgel* are an anachronism. They are given over to elegance and frivolity and are governed not by material necessity but by ceremonial, traditional rites. Radiguet mocked those critics who would have liked him at least to divulge the color of his heroine's eyes in *Devil in the Flesh.*[19] In his second novel, material reality is even less substantial. We find almost no details about the characters' appearance. While much time is spent around a table, in the course of lunches and dinners, no information is given about what is eaten. The very settings are almost insubstantial: no description of house interiors, or for that matter of external sites, other than the most rudimentary, schematic notations. In addition, with the exception of Paul Robin, whom we know to be a diplomat, none of the characters is or feels any need to be employed gainfully. Even Paul Robin's work does not keep him from his—more important—pleasures, and we are given no details about what his work entails. Radiguet appears so determined to reject the reified world of naturalism and realism that he systematically withholds descriptions of things, or declines to identify them. For example, the dressing room of the Fratellini clowns at the Medrano circus is filled with items; but, tantalizingly, the narrator does not tell us what they are, only that they no longer serve the purpose for which they were first made. In the clowns' room, "grandiose, unclaimed objects had come to rest, objects stripped of their original meaning and which now, taken over by these clowns, assumed a much nobler one" (*B*, 27).[20]

The Ball

Inevitably, the reader's attention, in the absence of things upon which to focus, is concentrated upon the characters. In the absence of physical traits or significant actions from these characters, it is concentrated upon their temperament or character, upon who they are and not upon what they do: in a word, upon their essence rather than their existence. The ball, featured in Radiguet's title, is a perfect conceit for this authorial viewpoint.

In *The Princess of Cleves,* it is at the royal ball at the Louvre that the heroine encounters the Duke de Nemours and first awakens to the possibility of love. The king calls upon the newly married Mme de Cleves to dance with the Duke de Nemours. First individually, then dancing together as a couple, the duke and the princess are the center of attention for all those present:

When she appeared that evening, everyone wondered at her beauty and the elegance of her attire. The ball opened; while she was dancing with Monsieur de Guise, there was a commotion near the door of the ballroom, as though people were stepping aside to let someone enter. Mme de Cleves finished the dance. As she was looking around for her next partner, the king summoned her to dance with the gentleman who had just entered. On looking round, she saw a man making his way around the chairs to the dance-floor. Immediately she thought of Monsieur de Nemours. This prince was strikingly handsome: without ever having seen him before, one would notice him, especially this evening, since he had taken pains to look his attractive best, to enhance further his already distinguished mien.

It was difficult to meet Mme de Cleves also for the first time without being impressed. Monsieur de Nemours was struck by her beauty. When she curtsied in response to his arrival, he could not conceal his great admiration. They began to dance. Murmurs of praise went through the ballroom.[21]

Before Radiguet, many other writers, including Stendhal, Balzac, Flaubert, and Proust, had made of the ball a central scene in their novels. Radiguet, however, rings a change on the subject. Early in the novel, there is of course the dance at the Robinson, at which François yearns to take Mahaut in his arms. Here, as in *The Princess of Cleves,* a ball opens the action and is a concentrated metaphor for what follows. But the principal ball is not actually presented within the narrative: it is projected for a later date, after the novel ends. The ball, in *Count d'Orgel,* is not so much an event as it is a metaphor for the lives of the characters who are presented. The ball suggests movement, elegance, set rules, and repetition. Partners come together, separate, change, and may come together once more. Underlying the whole spectacle is the notion of design or pattern: rhythm, repetition, recurrence. But, in the assemblage of participants, there is still room for chance encounter, unforeseeable circumstance. An unusual feature of the ball, moreover, is that it is gratuitous: it is not end-oriented; it does not aim to accomplish anything or attain any objective. But it does reveal character, and the opportunities for observation of character are considerable. Paradoxically, this is as true of the masked ball, where inhibitions drop, as of any other; to borrow a remark of Cocteau's: "It is a fact that the masked ball unmasks."[22]

Radiguet's characters perform their elegant or frivolous movements with no ultimate objective in mind: they are gratuitous. They appear to act freely, although they do respect strict conventions and, of a common accord, are bound by tight rules of etiquette. In fact, to a large extent, even when they believe they are acting freely, they are repeating patterns that have already been enacted. In other words, a form of fatality—not ponderous but subtle—weighs upon them. It is scarcely an exaggeration to say that, in the case of Radiguet's characters, essence precedes existence: they do not improvise their steps in the dance to the music of time: they follow them.[23]

Time and Character

Within *Count d'Orgel* there are two time-frames, not one. The actual events take place over an eight-month period. It is too easy to ignore the fact that the characters' conduct in this period is very much conditioned and colored by the past: not just their own, but their ancestors', a historical past. This forms a second, essential time-frame. One critic, failing to perceive this, asserts that "the first pages of the novel, on the origin of the Grimoard [Mahaut's family] are hardly comprehensible and strike us as being without a real connection with the remainder of the narrative."[24] Mahaut, as we see her, has nothing in common with the existentialist protagonist, self-created and free; instead, she is the latest in a line, the depository of traits that have been transmitted over hundreds of years. Her voice is that of her race, for example, as her husband's is that of his:

Her speech had something harsh about it; graceful but stern, it appeared rough, masculine to the uninitiated. More than features, voice reveals race. The same kind of naiveté would have led people to think Anne's voice effeminate. His was a family voice, a voice that is still to be found in the theater. (*B, 29*)

The very differences that set her apart temperamentally from her husband are not individual differences, but ancestral; whereas she belongs to the feudal, landed aristocracy, he is the scion of a family that had always been at court. His perception of reality is limited to what happens in public; his greatest fear is of scandal, and there is in fact a world of difference between him and his wife: all the difference between Versailles (his natural habitat) and a medieval feudal castle (hers). As a result, her seriousness, like his frivolity, are inherited traits, shared by their respective families.[25] It becomes clear, then, that the first pages of the novel are anything but irrelevant or extraneous. In fact, if one looks closely enough, it may be possible to predict an unhappy fate for Mahaut after the actual conclusion of the novel. One of her ancestors was Josephine. She, like Mahaut, had gone to France from Martinique. Her unhappiness in marriage (first with the Viscount Beauharnais, then with Napoleon) may well be construed as prefiguring Mahaut's own misfortune in love.

Mahaut is not the only character for whom the past shapes the present. The very first mention of Anne d'Orgel in the novel underlines not his appearance or "individuality," but his name, "a fairly good name in France" (*B, 23*). This sets the pattern of a man who inherits the past and displays it in his thoughts and deeds. He impresses those who come into contact with him, and this faculty stems from his race: "his qualities were just those of his race" (*B*, 23). The perfect courtier in a century without a king, Anne remains comfortable only when he is surrounded by people, in the artificial atmosphere that prevailed at court: "It was not a lack of heart, but Anne d'Orgel was at ease only in an artificial atmosphere, in the blinding light of a room full of people" (*B*, 70). Such a man brings to bear upon life a perspective unlike that of another. Like the courtier at Versailles in the seventeenth century, Anne considers conversation an art of the highest importance, at its best a "masterpiece" (*B*, 74). His childlike joy in preparing for the masked ball is no merely personal idiosyncrasy; the preparatory activities "awoke in Anne the most profound passion of the men of his class through the centuries: that of disguise" (*B*, 179). We come to realize that differences that have been centuries in the making open a huge gap in understanding between Anne and Mahaut. Her passion elicits no equivalent response in him. At first, she had fallen passionately in love with Anne. He is a stranger to intimacy, and it is only when he sees his wife with François, at a distance, as it were, or as "another" woman, that he comes to love her: "That day her husband had longed for her as though she were not his wife" (*B*, 88). At the end, Mahaut is appalled by her passion for François, for she fears its radical consequences, whereas Anne's concern is only to maintain appearances, to act as if nothing untoward had occurred.

It would not be extreme to assert that Radiguet, in *Count d'Orgel*, presents a race or class theory of psychology. He does so without solemnity, invokes no scientific theory to justify his point of view, and is extremely deft in his presentation of character. The portraits are more reminiscent of a seventeenth-century moralist such as La Bruyère—especially since Radiguet also makes much use of the maxim, a common classical device—than they are of sketches by Balzac, Taine, Zola, or any other "scientific" determinists. Nonetheless the author applies his theory or technique consistently across the board, to all of the characters. François, for example, is granted access to noble houses because of a certain family air of nobility. Neither he nor his hosts are consciously aware of this: but it exists. His mother, for her part, thinks that she behaves like a woman of the middle class. But her noble origins transpire in her deeds in spite of herself, *noblesse oblige:* "Associating only with them, Mme de Séryeuse finally adopted the prejudices of the old bourgeoisie against the aristocracy without realizing that she was condemning her own people. Nonetheless she was forever acting in a way that revealed her breeding" (*B*, 75).

Among the relatively minor characters also, ancestry will out. Princess Hortense d'Austerlitz owes her gusto and common touch to her family antecedents: she was of recent nobility, that created by Napoleon, while earlier her family had been butchers. The Persian prince, Mirza, reveals his race involuntarily: "His race would emerge when one least expected it" (*B*, 112). Similarly, although Naroumov's sensitivity is shaped by the suffering he has known, it is also a product of his origins (*B*, 183).

The least sympathetic portrayals in the novel are reserved for the two commoners, Paul Robin and Hester Wayne. Whereas all of the others are very much "children" of the *ancien régime*—prerevolutionary times—these two are not provided with a substantial past. Paul is a product of the nineteenth century and, claims the narrator, more's the pity. A rather ridiculous descendant of Rastignac or of Julien Sorel,[26] Paul is a social climber, eager to succeed, to see and be seen: "Unburdened of all that foolish literature, a production of the nineteenth century, how charming he might have been" (*B*, 25). We know nothing of Hester Wayne's childhood or parents, let alone her more distant ancestry. She is repeatedly described as the "American woman" (*B*, 45, 46, 48). She is a shrill, vulgar seductress, a negative counterpoint to Mahaut's purity. She is thought beautiful by her contemporaries, but the narrator considers this assessment to be flawed, a misperception. By implication, the aesthetic standards of the time—1920—are not to be trusted. A truer beauty is that of François's mother, who at thirty-seven "looked like French women of the sixteenth century" (*B*, 78). In a vulgar age, however, it is Hester Wayne and not Mme de Séryeuse who is found attractive by the majority.

Underlying Radiguet's character portrayal is a rather deep pessimism, which shows itself in a number of ways. The very element of fatality implied by the weight of the past upon the present is in itself pessimistic. Radiguet's characters, laden with their ancestry, are far from being free agents. Throughout the novel, there is a pattern of unhappiness, especially in marriage. Indeed, there is in *Count d'Orgel* no example of a long, lasting, loving marital relationship.[27] Some of the marital misfortunes stretch the reader's credulity. For example, not only is the Persian prince Mirza a widower, but even his fifteen-year-old niece has been widowed.

The world in miniature represented by the Count d'Orgel and his entourage, noble, elitist conservators of the past, is shown to be threatened and vulnerable in the novel. Naroumov is the best illustration of the ruin that threatens. He loses everything in the Bolshevik Revolution and now cuts a pathetic if moving figure. Much earlier, the French Revolution had led to Napoleon and the sudden elevation of thousands of commoners to the nobility: "This outlandish masquerade, when people changed names as readily as one puts on a false nose, wounded them" (*B*, 20). On the very edge of this society, threatening to encroach still further upon it and eventually to cause it to disappear, is the larger, leveling society of the people. It is presented strikingly when the count and his friends, heading out of Paris for the Robinson dancing establishment, are obliged to stop at the porte d'Orléans when a car breaks down. A crowd is lined up outside: "A procession of cars was waiting to start up again. . . . The gaping people who made up this impudent line pressed their noses against the windows of the vehicles, so as to take a better look at their owners. The women pretended to find this ordeal charming" (*B*, 35). While there is no real danger in this encounter, it is one of several episodes showing the huge gap between the classes.

When set alongside let us say *The Conquerors* (1928), by André Malraux, *Count d'Orgel* strikes us as an extraordinarily reactionary novel. Malraux's characters come to life in or date from the turbulence of the historical present: "A general strike is ordered in Canton."[28] How far is Radiguet from this conception! His characters are antihistorical and anachronistic. They, petrified in the present, are heirs to the past; indeed, they are little more than filters or foci through which the past is allowed to seep. In a sense, the action is reaction, for it is a denial of the present and of history since the French Revolution. The diachronic sequence—the eight months of the foreground action—is accompanied by the indispensable, synchronic, and analeptic weight of the past. Each character is an heir, drawing consciously or unwittingly, for good or ill, upon the tradition he or she embodies.

Radiguet wrote *Count d'Orgel* when he was in contact with a number of partisans of the extreme right-wing movement known as *Action Française*, and the conclusion appears inescapable that such intercourse helped shape the values that underpin his novel.

Count d'Orgel is by no means obtrusively ideological. The fiction carries its ideas and values, or is borne by them, gracefully. The philosophical statement does not stand out as ungainly excrescence or awkward digression, as it does in some of the novels of the Goncourt brothers, or even certain works by Sartre, for example. Instead, it is assimilated into the work, to be an implicit part of it. In its major features, however, it is a more subtle, less forthright echo of much of the conservative doctrine enunciated by Charles Maurras, the leading figure of the very influential *Action Française.*

In part, Maurras's profound antipathy toward revolution, and the French Revolution especially, was based upon his complete devotion to the past. Whereas the revolutionary wished to eradicate the past, in order to start anew, Maurras repeatedly voiced his ardent desire to revalidate the prerevolutionary past, and not repudiate it. Repeatedly he underlined the fact that man is an heir and exhorted his fellow countrymen not to forget the past: "Do not forget: that is the point of departure of all order and of all law."[29] By the same token, he loathed the "revolutionary Beast,"[30] which brought anarchy in its tracks. Maurras believed strongly in immutable essences, immutable nature, and in particular in unchanging, essential human nature. In social terms, this expressed itself in an advocacy of rank and hierachy, and a belief in the hereditary aristocracy. Authority, in Maurras's words, "is born."[31] The quality of the leading class was grounded specifically in its rank; so, he wished above all to reintroduce and enforce this rank and hierarchy. Maurras was very distrustful of the nineteenth century and its ideals, from democracy to competitiveness and ambition. He was equally distrustful of foreign influences, be they American, German, or Jewish.[32]

While Radiguet does not go so far as to advocate the return of the monarchy—as Maurras does—and does not show the same antipathy toward foreigners—and Germans in particular—as Maurras, his characters in *Count d'Orgel* embody many of Maurras's principal ideas. Their lives are colored, shaped, and conditioned by those of their forebears, to whom an indelible, straight line connects them. Radiguet's commitment, like that of Maurras, is to an essentialist psychology: that is, his characters' essence is very real and precedes their existence. Radiguet is as far from existentialism as possible. Similarly, he is as far removed as possible from a Balzac or a Stendhal. His characters have nothing in common with the strenuous, striving, struggling, and scheming end-oriented activities of a Vautrin, a

Julien Sorel, or a Rastignac, viewing Paris as a possible booty. The two exceptions in *Count d'Orgel,* Paul Robin and Hester Wayne, who are deprived of a past, are condemned to be free in a different sense from that proposed by Sartre. They do not achieve lucidity and dignity accompanied by anguish; on the contrary, lacking tradition and lineage as a guide, heirs to no long and legitimate tradition, they are misguided, arbitrary, and simply wrong in their values, opinions, and judgments.

Within the context of Radiguet's apparent conservatism, his assessment of the novel of love as "profoundly, gravely frivolous"[33] is more than a superficial *boutade.* Applying himself to the analysis of feelings, and not external events, success, or ambition, he gives his characters the opportunity to reveal these feelings. By our contemporary standards of goal-setting, the pursuit of material well-being, and the striving after power or success, the activities in which the Count d'Orgel and his companions indulge are frivolous, of little consequence or importance. But, insofar as these characters escape these contemporary standards and hark back to a much earlier period, their activities are appropriate to them, reveal them in their essence, and are, accordingly, important. This "frivolity" is a less structured, more informal, but equally revealing equivalent of the ball: the paradigm of the life led by an exclusive group whose roots are in the customs of the *ancien régime.*

Chapter Five

Radiguet Critic of His Time: The Aesthetics

As critic or commentator, Radiguet is not well known, and this is not very surprising. Within his own lifetime he published only a handful of short articles, of which almost half were reviews of works by Cocteau. After his death, a very substantial body of criticism was discovered and eventually published. However, these commentaries, ranging over an extraordinarily wide field of topics, are often schematic in nature, taking the form of notes, tentative outlines, incomplete reminiscences, fragmentary comments. It may even appear presumptuous to talk about Radiguet's "aesthetics," in view of the early age at which he died and the apparent variousness of his response. However, Radiguet's response to the intellectual and artistic questions of his time was thoughtful, intense, and even passionate, and it is possible to find in his writing the outlines of a cogent and consistent aesthetic program. Like Gide or Mauriac or Breton, Raymond Radiguet was aware of living in a crucial period, a time of crisis and transition, when an older order had been destroyed or mortally wounded, and a newer one not yet created. No writer was closer to the manifold currents that flowed through his period than Radiguet. Having first been caught up in them, he then tried to steer his own course and find his own artistic and intellectual direction. His critical writings, fragmentary though they may be, help us better to understand the cultural climate immediately after World War I, and add considerably to our understanding of Radiguet, who is otherwise so enigmatic.

The Period

The aftermath of the destruction wrought by the war was, inevitably, a calling into question of the very wellsprings of human motivation and activity: an attempt, often a desperate attempt, to understand. It was current practice to talk of a new *mal du siècle*. A fundamental sense of unease or anxiety—*l'inquiétude*—was so widespread as to have become a cliché: "the merest reader of the avant-garde journals thought himself stricken with fervor, then with anxiety."[1] This profound disquiet, brought on by the loss of values resulting from the sheer hideousness and perceived absurdity of the war, was considered the outstanding characteristic of a whole generation—"Anxiety has become a fashion: without anxiety, no fine soul, no literary talent, even,"[2]—and is revealed in some of the titles of novels from the period: *L'Inquiète Adolescence,* by Chadourne, *L'Enfant Inquiet,* by Obey, or Lacretelle's *La Vie Inquiète de Jean Hermelin.*[3]

For intellectuals on the left, the whole edifice of traditional beliefs, from God to country, family, and the notion of progress, no longer offered shelter against despair, dissolution, and the immanence of death; the whole structure, with its political, religious, and social conventions, needed to be rebuilt. For many, nothing short of a revolution could cure the ills of the country. The intellectuals of the right, on the other hand, were equally convinced of living in a time of discredited values, but saw as the cure not a revolutionary leap into the future but rather a reactionary return to the past. They advocated an adoption of the elitist traditions going back to pre-revolutionary France, to "old France," and felt that the contemporary, spiritual anarchy stemmed from the French Revolution, which had spawned the evils of egalitarianism and democracy.[4]

Some sixty years later, it is difficult to grasp the intensity with which the crisis of the period was experienced, and the depth of feeling it stirred up. But there was indeed a radical split between the advocates of revolution on the one hand—a heterogeneous range of figures from the political heirs of Jaurès to the dadaists—and, on the other, those articulate champions of reaction and integral nationalism who followed Charles Maurras under the banner of *Action Française.* Expressed simplistically and in understated terms, the war had formed a divide between the latter-day romantics on the left and their classical antagonists on the right. The centennial of Lamartine's *Méditations Poétiques* stirred a critic to write somewhat euphemistically, in 1920: "For you are not unaware that today the struggle between classicism and romanticism is almost as lively as a century ago."[5]

Max Jacob

Radiguet claimed to be immune to the anxiety that was the characteristic of this generation and was perhaps best symbolized by the extreme popularity, at the time, of the novels of Dostoyevski. Like many another writer before and since, he claimed to chart an independent course. However, having plunged into the artistic life of Paris in 1918, Radiguet was inevitably and of necessity subject to its crosscurrents. The first major influence upon him, one that was to leave its mark for the remainder of his years, was Max Jacob. Although circumstances came to separate them, Radiguet remained constant in his high regard for the author of *Le Cornet à dés:*

Dramatist, poet, short-story writer, novelist and even painter, Max Jacob is good at everything he tackles. I think that his influence on the young is even greater than that of Guillaume Apollinaire. He has introduced a new sensitivity into poetry. It would be a profound error just to take him for a poet of whimsy. I do not know any book more serious than *Le Cornet à dés.*[6]

Initially Radiguet and Max Jacob saw each other constantly. Gradually, however, as the younger writer came under Cocteau's protection, their meetings grew less frequent. Jacob would complain, "Radiguet no longer comes to see me."[7] With Jacob's retreat to the monastery of St.-Benoît sur Loire, they saw each other still less. But Jacob was eager to maintain contact, considering Radiguet to be his friend. He asked a correspondent to bear a greeting on his behalf: "Do say hello to my friends. To that fine man Satie, to the scholar Malraux, to the young Radiguet."[8] While Radiguet was far from being the most constant of friends, it is clear that he did undergo Jacob's influence.

In some instances, Jacob's importance to the development of Radiguet's own work is abundantly clear. It was thanks to Jacob that Radiguet was exposed to cubism and came into contact with artists of the younger generation, such as Breton, Reverdy, or Gris. Some of Radiguet's techniques in his earlier poetry, such as recurring punning and the use of a kind of protean imagery involving a succession of changing planes of meaning, justified logically by the slimmest of connections, owe much to Jacob's work. Radiguet's first published work, a lighthearted presentation of Parisian characters in the Métro entitled "Galanterie Française," appears to borrow heavily from Jacob, with a youth called Toto, like a character in *Le Cornet à dés,*[9] and the stereotypical *titi parisien,* or street arab. In other instances, however, Jacob's "presence" is more elusive, subtle, and lasting, and much more important.

Unlike Cocteau, and much more than Apollinaire, Jacob never allowed himself to forget the long literary tradition that lay behind him. Unusually innovative himself, he delighted, with great eccentricity, in calling himself a reactionary and a foe of avant-garde "disorder." Proud of having reinvented the prose poem, he nonetheless insisted upon his own sense of structure and tradition:

. . . my favorite manuscript . . . is the manuscript of my prose poems, a genre that I have set free from the picturesque tableaux of Aloysius Bertrand, from the Baudelairean parable, or that of Mallarmé, from the disorderly impressionism of Rimbaud and his followers, in order to bring it closer to the rigorous composition of Japanese poems or Spanish jotas. This very thick manuscript is preceded by a preface in which I recall the harm done by Rimbaud to style, that is, to traditional composition. I am a reactionary. Revolutions are carried out only by remembering the past.[10]

In spite of his friendship with Picasso, Gris, Reverdy, and Breton, and notwithstanding his own extraordinarily original creations, Jacob claimed to be classical and insisted that he was not fond of his own age. Like Charles Maurras, he railed against the nineteenth-century tradition in art: "Rimbaud represents the disorder that I abhor," and "I loathe naturalism, realism, and any work that makes its point only through the comparison one makes between it and real life."[11] In addition, although Jacob was born a Jew, he claimed to admire Gobineau, who was among other things the founder of an anti-Semitic race theory that Charles Maurras accepted. Jacob admired Ronsard and Racine and saw their Catholicism as a major factor in their greatness; in Jacob's eyes, at least, Racine's Jansenism did not apparently make him any less orthodox! On the other hand, he had no sympathy at all for the complexities of Dostoyevski: "Religion does not like Dostoyevski's gibberish."[12]

Perhaps the most remarkable fact about the opinions held, or at least uttered, by Jacob is that they all date from 1917 or earlier, some years before the "return to classicism" for which Cocteau took—and was given—credit. Radiguet, for his part, in his first, published critical essay, on Juan Gris, calls the painter a "classic," stresses that Gris can find beauty in everyday, familiar objects, and admires his sense of proportion. Jacob may well have been an important influence on Radiguet when he first began his career. Certainly, in his later adoption of conventional models and his respect for the French tradition, Radiguet took up a position very close to that formulated by Jacob, and the influence of the Breton poet seems undeniable. There was to be, however, between these two phases a change of direction, a long interlude in the course of which Radiguet drew very close to Breton and that group, sympathetic to dada, which had grown up around the journal *Littérature*.

The Association with Breton

From the beginning, Breton respected Radiguet highly and showed no esteem for Cocteau. He was eager to find space in his new journal for the writing of Radiguet, but, being deeply doubtful of Cocteau's seriousness, studiously excluded him. In a letter to Tzara in January 1919, Philippe Soupault, Breton's associate, cites Radiguet's name alongside that of Aragon, Breton himself, and a few others as being that of a writer "of great talent."[13] Throughout 1919, until the beginning of 1920, Breton and Radiguet were on very close terms. Breton published several of his pieces, and the tone of Radiguet's letters reveals his willingness to unburden himself to the other. He complains, for example, about the ironic stares that greet him at the Certa bar, the dadaist headquarters, states his dislike for Louis Aragon, and even, in one letter, confesses that he finds *Les Champs Magnétiques* (Magnetic fields), an experiment in automatic writing by Breton and Soupault, boring.[14] When Radiguet was invited, along with others among "the most qualified representatives of the diverse tendencies of contemporary literature,"[15] to respond to the question "Why do you write?" he replied very much along the lines of Breton's "creed." At a time when gratuitousness—unmotivated action—was much in vogue, and Lafcadio, its representative in Gide's *Les Caves du vatican,* was an object of fascination for Breton's group, Radiguet answered succinctly: "I was awaiting your question in order to identify with Lafcadio. *Without reason* he commits a crime: all the more reason to consider him to be not without seriousness." Claiming therefore that his writing is unmotivated, Radiguet concludes his piece by saying: "Rather, ask your readers: Why do *you read?*"[16]

Breton appears to have been impressed by Radiguet's talents and his seriousness. Gradually, however, the character of *Littérature* became more polemic, in effect demanding a commitment for and against persons and causes; as a result, it grew more and more restrictive in its sympathies and bellicose in its dislikes. For Tzara, Rilke was no more than a "sentimental and rather stupid poet," while Proust was described as a "laborious snob."[17] Although both Radiguet and Jacob had pieces appear in *Littérature* as late as February 1920, a split had already appeared between them and Breton before this date. Later that year, Cocteau, in whose company Radiguet could always be found, was violently attacked in *Littérature,* his *Carte Blanche* articles being compared by Benjamin Péret to the spilled contents of a trash-can!

I empty my trash-cans. You empty your trash-cans. He empties his trash-cans, etc. All year long, he has done that, but as he is too lazy to take them down and empty them on the side-walk, he throws them out the window. . . . I spotted a pile of soiled papers on the ground: on one of them was written *Carte Blanche.* I looked up. He was still emptying his trash-cans.[18]

Littérature took a direction radically different from that espoused by Radiguet. In May 1920, it published twenty-three dada manifestos, describing—and advocating—dada as a state of mind comprising "perpetual revolution," "anti-art," and "free instinct." To a large extent, over the next year or so, Radiguet's aesthetics would be formulated in complete opposition or contradistinction to the ideas put forward by Breton's group. *Littérature* made itself the champion of the creative role of free, uninhibited chance and instinct: ". . . to make a dadaist poem: Take a newspaper. / Take some scissors. . . ."[19] It attacked all and any thinking in the rational tradition of Descartes, saying of the philosopher Alain, for example, "He drivels,"[20] and publishing articles such as the one by Aragon entitled "Down with the Clear French Genius."[21] Its growing seriousness took it far beyond the theatrics of dada, and the inevitable break with Tzara and dada was eventually consecrated in April 1922, when Breton published his article "Drop Everything," advocating a break with family, friends, children, mistress, and . . . dada!

The differences that grew up between Breton and Radiguet are obvious. Breton never relented in his hatred for establishment, tradition, and convention: values that Radiguet came to adopt. Nonetheless there was common ground between the two, not just at Radiguet's debut but even later, when their differences were greatest. There was, in the first place, their shared seriousness about their mission and their discontent with the nineteenth century. Both were concerned with the need to find and found a new mythology of the contemporary world and believed that the old myths or symbols had lost their meaning or resonance. Before either of them, Jacob had been preoccupied by the same need. But this common sense of a need for renewal led Breton "out to sea," to travel the surrealist adventure, whereas Radiguet opted to stay closer to home, linking up with an old French tradition, opting for a form of conservative reaction.

The Break with Breton and his Group.
Enter Jean Cocteau

In 1920, the very volume of activities among the leaders of the avant-garde, along with their stridency, and some shifting of allegiance, led to confusion as to who belonged to which group. It was sometimes claimed—indeed, it still is—that Cocteau was a cubist or a dadaist. One critic asserted that Cocteau was a cubist before Apollinaire! He claimed that Cocteau and his fellow cubists loved Paris but were also fervent travelers, fond of depicting "voyages, large express trains, large steamboats, ships' telegraphs," and the United States.[22] In point of fact, this particular Fregoli-like transformation was behind Cocteau. To be sure, he had indeed, in the wake of Cendrars and Apollinaire—not before them—sung the praises of cityscape and distant travel. In 1920, however, he was poised ready for another quick change. Throughout the year, the refrain he made his own was "Farewell, New York!" In this most active of years for dadaists, when a critic could comment, "In short, 1920 will have been their year,"[23] Breton's steadfast hatred for Cocteau quite prevented the latter from joining the group. Instead, Radiguet joined forces with Cocteau, and the two became inseparable. At a time when Picasso, independently, was beginning to step out in high society, Cocteau opened the doors of Parisian high life to his protégé. Automatically, Radiguet incurred the intense displeasure of Breton, for whom any friend of Cocteau's was an enemy.

It is impossible to know for certain whether Radiguet was "sincere" in his adoption of a new, classical approach to literature or whether he was motivated by self-interest in following Cocteau. In any case, once he had adopted a conservative or traditional strategy, he was entirely consistent in following it. His political, literary, and aesthetic tastes were first adumbrated, and then, converging into a coherent pattern, enunciated and followed. From 1920 on, Radiguet presents a viewpoint that sees the present as a continuation and renewal of the past, rather than a break with it. The movement in this direction was initiated by Cocteau, who had no doubt come under the influence of Jacob and others. As early as 1918, in his essay on music, *Le Coq et l'Arlequin,* Cocteau had advocated French music, free of foreign influences. In 1920, he returned to the rose as his emblem, linking up with a tradition going back at least as far as Ronsard. But Cocteau's brand of "classicism" or traditionalism was anything but consistent. While coming, in contradistinction to dada, to proclaim order over anarchy, and his approval of tradition over revolution, and so on, Cocteau was extraordinarily idiosyncratic in his understanding of classical or traditional norms. Radiguet, on the other hand, was more consistent; he, unlike Cocteau, appears to have thought his position through. There is good reason to consider that, although Cocteau turned Radiguet in the direction of classicism, it was Radiguet himself who took this change seriously, thought out his artistic attitude carefully, and adhered to it, becoming in turn his mentor's mentor!

By December 1919 Radiguet had taken the first steps toward a position diametrically opposed to that of the future surrealists. From July of that year on, Jacques Doucet had commissioned from the young man some literary essays. In December he wrote a laudatory piece on Cocteau in which he stressed the latter's very French qualities. Radiguet's rejection of internationalism in art is clearly a rebuttal of dada, which passionately hated nationalism. He writes:

> Among all the poets, Jean Cocteau seems to me to have brought into play that nimble wit which is most French.
> People say: arts knows no frontiers. A self-evident lie! A land of artists such as ours gains nothing from such fallacious internationalism. [24]

Radiguet questions whether the miracle of the Marne could have occurred in any country but France and affirms that the three syllables of Jean Cocteau's name resound very like a French flag beating in the wind.

Before long, Radiguet's literary and artistic interests ran completely counter to those of the dadaists. In 1919 he had mentioned Alfred Jarry in rather neutral terms. Jarry's iconoclasm made him of course a favorite of Breton's band. But, by the spring of 1920, Radiguet lumped together Jarry, the dadaists, and, for good measure, added Oscar Wilde, Gide's creation Lafcadio, and the painter Francis Picabia, condemning all of them in no uncertain terms:

> I hate Bohemian life. I find pranks a pain, and, for these two reasons, the account of Alfred Jarry's life would not enrapture me.
>
> By reviving mystification, dada draws nearer to the worst of Bohemian life: that part leading to Incoherence.
>
> Dada is a cul-de-sac; the route leading to it is Oscar Wilde–André Gide (Wilde's mission of demoralization and, much more recently, Gide's Lafcadio).
>
> The dadaists secretly cherished paradox. In public, they call that "the right to contradict oneself."
>
> If the arts were not *inevitably* innocuous, of all public hazards, the work of Francis Picabia would be the worst. . . .
>
> Dada is a label. What does the bottle contain? A harmless drink that the dadaists would have us believe is a deadly poison.[25]

Radiguet's opinions were undoubtedly shaped by Cocteau's strained relations not only with Breton but also with Picabia. Picabia had, in rather devious fashion, kept Cocteau's poems out of *391,* while making public a *lettre de rupture* from Cocteau in the new anarchist journal *Cannibale.* Moreover, Radiguet's article loses a little of its sting if one recalls that it was not published until after his death. Nonetheless his tone is trenchant, and he systematically repudiates everything that Breton and Tzara held dear. For example, the very reference to mystification ("By reviving mystification . . .") may appear anodyne. In fact, Breton's group took pride in mystifying the public, and, in an issue of *Littérature* (September 1919), a letter from Jacques Vaché to Louis Aragon—whom Radiguet disliked—begins: "Dear friend and Mystifier." In addition, both in this article and elsewhere, Radiguet denounces the dadaists' fondness for symbolist poetry. He points to the irony of their admiration for a school of poets, while they claimed allegiance to no school, and suggests that the symbolists' failings as artists undoubtedly derived from their being an international, rather than a national, group.

Articulated in this short article, "Dada or the Nothingness Bar,"[26] are a number of features that came to form the foundation of Radiguet's aesthetics. They were given fuller expression throughout 1920 and later, in both published and unpublished articles. Initially Radiguet may have made a virtue out of necessity, turning conservative because his friendship with Cocteau excluded him from the avant-garde. But the very consistency and sustained vigor with which he espoused this position, not to mention the creative works that put the principles to work, suggest that he was very comfortable indeed with the conservative strategy.

With the appearance of the little journal *Le Coq*, which had a brief but brilliant life, appearing in four issues in 1920, Cocteau and Radiguet had a platform from which to proclaim their rediscovery of the rose and their preference for works of "clarity, grace and balance" in the French tradition. Having seen himself denied access to *391*, Cocteau, with the financial backing of François Bernouard and the practical assistance of Radiguet, brought out his own equivalent of it. In *Le Coq*, the contrast between the medium and the message was striking, for the former was far from being the latter! Borrowing some of Picabia's visually striking ideas, including folded, colored paper, a telegraphic style reminiscent of advertising, and varied typographical setting, Cocteau and Radiguet advocated a respect for tradition, along with the rejection of modernity at any price!

If, for Cocteau, *Le Coq* represented an opportunity once more to surprise critic and reader, to try to hold center-stage, and to turn in a new direction, it was something more for Radiguet. He appears to have wished to assess the literary scene and his own position in relation to it. Cocteau's position was self-contradictory or at least ambiguous; for at the very moment he was bidding farewell to New York, he was staging his ballet-pantomine *Le Boeuf sur le toit*, which is set in a North American bar at the time of Prohibition and is in fact emphatically untraditional! Radiguet praises this production lavishly, but in this article as in two others he published in *Le Coq*, he takes a leaf out of Max Jacob's book, constantly juxtaposing past with present, mentioning Cocteau, Chaplin, or Apollinaire, but also stating his admiration for Racine or for Ronsard. Indeed each of his articles begins with a mention of a French literary figure of the past. While his style is light and bantering, the aesthetic principles he propounds are not far at all from those set out by Boileau, the codifier of seventeenth-century French classicism, in his *Art Poétique*. Radiguet makes a plea for simplicity in preference to complication, elegance and understatement over dishevelment and extravagance, the familiar in contradistinction to the bizarre. And, having seen the dadaists' pleasure in insulting the public, he insists upon respect for and acceptance by the public; Radiguet felt dismay that Aragon should wish to shock people.[27]

Radiguet's simultaneous apologia for Cocteau and for "classicism" was on occasion strained by the obvious disparity between the two. One example involves the restaging, in 1920, of Cocteau's "realist ballet" *Parade*. It had initially been conceived as an avant-garde spectacle, intended to create the "scandal" for which Cocteau had longed. Radiguet, in 1920, passes over Cocteau's delight in scandalizing the public in 1917 and claims that *Parade* is a work of extreme clarity, simplicity, accessibility, and understatement: the purveyor of profound truth, having much in common with Racine and nothing with Rimbaud. Furthermore Radiguet somehow claims that *Parade* is a truly French creation. In fact, it had been danced by the Russian ballets, with sets and costumes by Picasso, a Spaniard! Likewise, it is amply clear that Cocteau's *Les Mariés de la tour Eiffel* (The wedding party on the Eiffel Tower), recounting the misadventures that befall a very bourgeois wedding group on the first platform of the monument, was conceived as an enthusiastic, avant-garde production, in the mood of Apollinaire's *esprit nouveau*. But Radiguet chooses to emphasize in this spectacle Cocteau's ability to "endow contemporary things with an ancient character, a mythological one."[28] In defiance of Apollinaire, Delaunay, and others, who admired the Eiffel Tower as a thing of beauty in itself, as well as a break with the past, Radiguet asserts that the structure is intrinsically ugly: it is, he claims, by a tour de force on the part of Cocteau that it is made beautiful! For Radiguet, this poetic feat is akin to Ronsard's transformation of his plain mistress into a person of beauty, through the power of his verse. And Radiguet insists that, forced to choose between two trite poetic images, a modern fairground on one hand a house with olive trees on the other, he would opt for the latter.

While many of Radiguet's aesthetic pronouncements appear fragmentary, they do, when collected, present a rather cohesive point of view. He was intent upon distilling and decanting what the past, and the world around him, had to offer. As much as Breton and

Apollinaire, Radiguet scorned the realist or naturalist approach to art. He disliked the raw response of Antoine in the theater, was not fond of Balzac, and considered Stendhal vulgar. He took pleasure in being criticized for not giving in his novels an apparently central, realistic detail: for example, the color of his heroine's eyes in *Devil in the Flesh*.[29] Going much further, in fact, he provided practically no physical description of his characters in either of his novels! On the other hand, unlike Apollinaire, Tzara, or Breton, Radiguet stated firmly that the pursuit of the modern at all costs, the quest for the contemporary, was doomed to have no more than passing interest; locked in totally to its own historic moment, it would die with the passing of that moment. Refining this position, however, Radiguet did not reject his own period. Instead, like the Baudelaire of *Spleen de Paris,* Radiguet was convinced that the world around him was rich in poetry, or the marvelous. Beneath the fleeting contemporary, or the trivial, lurked that which was ancient, significant, highly poetic, or mythical: a reality of lasting significance. The choice was elected by the artist. However, there was nothing mystical, supernatural, or transcendental about the poetic distillation effected by the writer. Informing Radiguet's analyses are a skepticism and an irony that appear quite modern. For example, religion or a feeling for the divine have no place in his work. He notes: "Religion—dead today—and since Jesus—since there are no more miracles."[30] There is some belief in inexplicable fatality; for example, after recounting an incident witnessed in his childhood, he states: "Such lessons, such examples, command you to think of fatality."[31] But he resists the notion of transcendental mystery, firmly rejecting the symbolists' imprecision and their preoccupation with the Ideal.[32] His distrust of lofty sentiment extends from the rebuke he levels at the French Revolution, "Since 1789, they have forced me to think, and it has given me a headache,"[33] to a distrust of the benefits of distant travel:

A poet is always an explorer; each, after his fashion, goes around the world. To become immortal, it is sometimes sufficient to travel around one's room, or one's heart.

Not all poets have gone to New York; I know some who have lunch on the banks of the Marne.[34]

In the absence of the divine, or the sublime, from Radiguet's work, there is—perhaps concomitantly—a frequent sense of melancholy as the basic life-feeling of his age. Radiguet was not of course the first to underline this awareness; it is a dominant trait of Picasso's Blue Period, and a recurring preoccupation for Apollinaire. Radiguet detects it in the work of Cocteau. Referring to *Le Potomak,* he claims that Cocteau, its author, "without wanting to, has created a new melancholy, that of fairs, of fireworks when they cease."[35]

Inevitably, Radiguet's distrust of lofty thoughts is accompanied by a similar distrust of bombastic language: "Just as one gets tired of the sublime, so one tires of big words."[36] Instead, he advocates the presentation of familiar objects, local commonplaces, and banal language: "Try to be banal":[37] clarity, simplicity, and accessibility.

Radiguet's abandonment of free-verse forms for the classical octosyllabic line and his adoption of the traditional novel were a logical accompaniment to his aesthetic position from 1920 on. Radiguet's consistency extends even to his art criticism. He wrote an article lauding an Ingres exhibition put on by the Comte de Beaumont.[38] In it he claims that it is impossible to create something entirely new. Instead, the artist should present the novelty he wishes to embody in a way that allows it to be appreciated and accepted by the public. This reconciliation of old forms and new thoughts had been advocated much earlier by André Chénier, a favorite poet of Radiguet's. It is this quality that he claims to find and admire in Ingres and Racine, and to account for their greatness. On the other hand, he feels that the cubists are too brazen in failing to choose a worthy subject, in failing to respect harmonious proportions, and in failing to respect their public. Even though Picasso himself briefly underwent a "classical" phase, and painted in the style of Ingres for a time, Radiguet's repudiation of cubism, and his preference for the "clear composure and bourgeois probity"[39] of Ingres, is striking in view of his former, fast friendship with Juan Gris, and his own "cubist" beginnings as a poet.

Radiguet and the Right: *Action Française*

In frequenting Cocteau's group, which counted among its number the Comte de Beaumont, Paul Morand, and Georges Auric, Radiguet was brought face to face with the partisans of the right-wing movement known as *Action Française,* of which the leader was Charles Maurras (1868–1952), a figure of very considerable stature around

1920. A number of Cocteau's acquaintances—including Morand and Auric—were sympathetic to the ideas expressed by Maurras in his "little gray journal," *Action Française,* as well as in his numerous other studies of politics and literature, especially poetry. Cocteau himself liked to see himself as a tightrope walker, stepping out in solitude, separated from political or artistic factions. He claimed to follow his own "line," a highly personal form of anarchism. In fact, it would be more accurate to see in his conduct an unwillingness to be left out of any movement that appeared significant, accompanied by an incapacity for committing himself steadfastly to any single position. He had none of the political intransigence of some of his associates on the left or the right. Politically he was naive, guided by a mixture of innocence (or irresponsibility) and, to be sure, self-interest. In World War I he sang a hymn of praise to Marshal Joffre, then joined forces with the leftist avant-garde. In World War II, his relations with the occupying Germans were checkered, to say the least. In 1920, his friends were from the right, but he was most eager not to alienate the other friends he had on the left! Radiguet was in no wise as equivocal as his mentor, rejecting Cocteau's claim that the right was next to the left: "The right. Where Jean Cocteau was correct in creating the extreme right— and where he was wrong (the extremes touch). That has reality in words only. It was fear of stating: the right, pure and simple."[40]

François Mauriac described Radiguet as a young man raised in the left wing of letters who then turned to classicism. More accurately, or specifically, Radiguet was raised in the left wing of letters but then veered sharply to the right. This switch is adequately documented in his personal writings and had its effects on his thinking and creative works. It seems quite clear that Radiguet's quest for a stable position brought him very close to the ideas expressed by Charles Maurras.

France is of course the country of revolution. Breton, Aragon, and their friends never forgot this. But too often it is forgotten that, revolution breeding counterrevolution as night follows day, France is also a country of reaction. The Dreyfus Affair was the most striking illustration of conservative feeling, encompassing xenophobia, anti-Semitism, and a nostalgic harking back to a prerevolutionary, prerepublican period—the *ancien régime*—perceived as simpler, purer. But reaction did not disappear with the separation of church and state in 1905: in fact it still has not disappeared. Around 1920,

Action Française, railing against democratic ideals, was at the zenith of its power and prestige.

As much as the intellectuals on the left, Charles Maurras sought authentic values in a world that seemed to him to be degraded or debased by recent history. His too was a quest for authenticity, hedged around by complete pessimism concerning religion and the contemporary state of institutions. His search led him to a discovery of "integral nationalism." He pledged total dedication to "the goddess France" (an expression borrowed from André Chénier, a favorite poet of his).[41] Maurras's form of nationalism wished to dissociate France completely from the ideas and republican progeny of the French Revolution. Anachronistic and antihistorical, it followed the guidance of Bonald and de Maistre in viewing the revolution as radically evil and disastrous. Moreover, proffering his slogan "Reaction first!"[42] Maurras saw in republicanism the triumph of disorder and the degradation of France. He considered the postrevolutionary era, the nineteenth century and the first part of the twentieth, as an unfortunate period, and the Dreyfus Affair was for him symptomatic of the ills that had brought France to its knees. His tenacious anti-Semitism reflected his belief that Jewry was an international, cosmopolitan phenomenon bearing a threat to sacred, integral nationalism, related, in this respect at least, to international republicanism. Maurras advocated the restoration of the monarchy, insisting that the *ancien régime* had been for France a time of beauty, order, greatness, and even progress.

The literary preferences of Maurras cannot be divorced from his political ideas. As a staunch, articulate proponent of order against disorder, he exerted great influence. The editor-in-chief of the journal *Action Française,* Léon Daudet (the son of Alphonse Daudet), was very effective in enlisting the services of important writers and thinkers. For a time even André Malraux, Radiguet's contemporary, was attracted to Maurras and *Action Française.*[43] The admiration of Maurras for seventeenth-century French classicism was immense, and, while he expressed some partiality to certain French romantics, he condemned much of the movement for its lack of precision, its cosmopolitanism, and its penchant for grandiose, hyperbolic theme and expression. In Maurras's view, Chénier, who had died on the guillotine, a victim of the French Revolution, was the greatest French poet of the nineteenth century: "Chénier remains the greatest poet of the nineteenth century, which he dominates, governs, obsesses."[44] Maurras shared with Chénier the belief that Greek antiquity offered models of artistic and moral excellence.

Maurras's brand of extreme right-wing fervor, and love of France, was quite compatible with his impassioned plea for regionalism. He was an avid admirer of his native province, Provence, and a friend of Mistral, its "national" poet. This advocacy of the provinces is just one of many features shared by him and by Radiguet. Scattered throughout the latter's prose articles—especially those that appeared shortly after his death or had to await the publication of the *Oeuvres Complètes* to see the light of day—are many notations revealing the depth of his right-wing sympathies.

In his diffuse notes, Radiguet returns quite often to his fondness for the right, and hostility to the left, which he considers to be discredited:

At the end of the war, there was a political and literary left. *La Caravane* etc.

There can no longer be any avant-garde.

The literary left. There was a time when it was not ridiculous to say the left. Now, there cannot be anyone but the right.

The right, instead of being a dead entity has become a living one. Reactionaries of all times have come out on bottom. Today they will come out on top—explain the meaning of the word "reaction" . . .

The Socialist Party is dying.[45]

He even claimed that he would have been upset if *Devil in the Flesh* had been endorsed by the left: *"Devil in the Flesh.* I have told everyone that nothing would have caused me more pain than to be supported by the left. Fortunately no such thing occurred."[46]

It is commonplace in France to believe that the French Revolution and the example of Napoleon opened the doors of power to youth, on the basis of merit. But Radiguet affirms the opposite: ". . . under the *ancien régime* a young man of twenty could aspire to entering the loftiest portals. It is the Republic that has killed youth. Does one think of Mlle de Chartres's being fifteen?"[47] Radiguet expresses his distaste for the nineteenth century by describing it with exactly the same epithet used by Léon Daudet in his study *Stupid Nineteenth Century.*[48] An enigmatic note of Radiguet's reads: "Return to Louis 14."[49] There is nothing enigmatic or ambiguous about his impressions of the nineteenth-century writers Balzac or Stendhal. He deplored the main currents of romanticism and realism;

he believed that Balzac and Stendhal had harmed the novel of love: "The heroes of Stendhal, Balzac want to 'make it.' Their love hinders their 'making it' and vice-versa."[50] The preoccupation with money, with becoming rich, was for Radiguet an impoverishment of fiction: "For me, in being enriched, in the nineteenth century, the novel of love was impoverished, lost its purity."[51] Above all, Radiguet's literary sympathy was with the writers of the *ancien régime,* although he did exempt a few postrevolutionary artists, including Fromentin, Nerval, Gobineau, and de Maistre, from his general dismissal. Like Maurras, he appears to have seen a continuity from the Middle Ages to the Renaissance, rather than a rupture. He vigorously defended the Middle Ages against Cocteau's rather facile attack upon the period,[52] and had in mind a study of the fifteenth-century poet Charles d'Orléans. And he was unstinting in his praise of Ronsard, du Bellay, la Fontaine, Molière, and Racine. Mme de Lafayette's *La Princesse de Clèves* was of course a model for *Count d'Orgel.*

Maurras has been viewed as the moral assassin of the pacifist Socialist leader Jean Jaurès, who was shot to death in 1914, on his return from a meeting of the Socialist International.[53] Jean Jaurès, a bitter opponent of Charles Maurras, had been well known as an orator. Radiguet appeared to share the negative feelings about Jaurès harbored by his father, as well as by his friend Jean Hugo. In a diary, he notes:

Then the death of Jaurès. Jean Hugo states that he heard him once, and that it was grotesque. What would his role have been during the war? I recall a remark of my father's, which had so struck me. It's sad but [that makes] one less trafficker.[54]

A very important component in Radiguet's makeup was his love for his own region. This is a characteristic he shared with many figures from his own period, including Maurras. In Radiguet's case, his "patriotism" applies much more to his province, the Ile-de-France, and to his own area, the Marne, than to France at large. He was not without nationalist feeling, but it is in no way presented with the fervor of a Maurras. On the other hand, he becomes quite lyrical in speaking of provincial ties: "Provinces. The natural boundaries. The reason why Alsace must be French. It was inevitable that tourism, taking into account natural frontiers, should restore their value to the provinces."[55] In describing his own home province,

Radiguet endows it with, or finds in it, an essential presence, a density of meaning, a depth he finds nowhere else. In reading the eloquent descriptions to be found in the long, unfinished essay "Ile-de-France, Ile d'Amour" (Ile-de-France, island of love), the reader understands that for Radiguet, as for Maurras (or Barrès, for that matter), the substance of literature is inseparable from the land that "nourished" or shaped it. Some of the terms Radiguet uses to describe the Ile-de-France might equally be applied to his favored texts in literature; this is a landscape of elusive beauty, serene limpidity, featureless understatement, rather than sublime hyperbole:

. . . if this province is more filled with poetry than any in the world, it is also the one in which you can feel it the least. For it has no poetic handicaps; its local color, you might say, is to have none. Its landscapes are never sublime; they are not even always beautiful or moving, but they *are*, just as the most beautiful landscapes that I know in literature do not come from the romantics: *descriptions*. . . . Nowhere else, it seems to me, is there fresh water like that which you find in the Ile-de-France.[56]

In sum, the Ile-de-France is for Radiguet a "classical" landscape, a mysterious distillation or quintessence of what is most French and, according to Radiguet, a factor influencing his own literary choices: "The absence of poetry (for people) from the Ile-de-France is the absence of poetry that some took pleasure in ascribing to *Devil in the Flesh*."[57]

Radiguet was not completely uncritical of Maurras or *Action Française*, even if a number of his positions run parallel to theirs. Certainly he criticized Léon Daudet rather severely, alleging that Daudet, an opponent of the French Republic, was himself too much of a politician, and enjoyed its protection unjustly. In those places where he mentions Maurras, Radiguet tends to be quite neutral in his comments, although in one place he taxes him with being vulgar, albeit less so than Daudet: "Charles Maurras is better, though not admirable, but if he is vulgar, his vulgarity is of an era preceding that of Léon Daudet."[58] On the other hand, he offers advice to himself to follow a technique used by Maurras: "Do like Maurras, appendix to his books, the use of letters," and he is happy to see Jean Cocteau's name among those of the traditionalist writers favored by Maurras:

What are called the traditionalists were not then what they are now—tight barriers. Would you have seen Charles Maurras citing the name of Jean Cocteau? It matters little to me that this name is found next to that of mediocre men. The important thing is that it is there.

Each has gone out to meet the other.[59]

It seems abundantly clear that Radiguet's adoption of "classicism" from 1920 until his death was a much greater commitment than has generally been realized. It entailed a reassessment of all of his positions, literary, aesthetic, intellectual, and political. In this he differed from Cocteau, who tried throughout his life to avoid all the consequences of assuming a position. Cocteau sought the approval of both the public and the iconoclastic avant-garde, both the left and the right. Such was his versatility that he could constantly change his positions according to the fashion of the day. Cocteau's adoption of "classicism" was just one more milestone on his long artistic itinerary. Radiguet was different.

The choice that Radiguet came to make, with consistency and almost daunting determination, was for the right wing: the conservative—indeed, the reactionary—end of the literary and political spectrum. By a curious irony, it may have been Max Jacob, self-proclaimed traditionalist, Jew, and eventual victim of fascism, who first sowed the seed of this attitude. Out of deference to Jacob, perhaps, or for whatever reason, Radiguet's writings are not tainted with the anti-Semitism of *Action Française*. In many other respects, however, Radiguet's point of view was close to that of Maurras. One can only guess in what directions his intellectual development might have led, had he lived on.

Chapter Six
Conclusion

The start of the new century into which Raymond Radiguet was born brought with it an eagerness for change, a sense of excitement, the promise—and eventually the fulfillment—of a quite new artistic vision, breaking with the tradition going all the way back to classicism and, before it, the Renaissance. Standing at center stage, among the leaders of this new vision, is Picasso, and summing up his extraordinary achievement is his masterly *Les Demoiselles d'Avignon,* ushering in cubism, pointing to the future, and self-consciously breaking with the past. Standing by Picasso's side were his friends the writers, among them the poets Apollinaire and Jacob, and the chronicler of the arts André Salmon. Each, in his way, affected Radiguet's development as a writer.

At about the time of *Les Demoiselles d'Avignon,* 1907, Picasso and his companions were acutely aware of reshaping the arts. Jacob could state to Salmon, with characteristic irony, but, at the same time, pride and self-confidence: "They must have told you about Racine, La Fontaine, and Boileau. Well, now it's our turn."[1]

Radiguet had barely turned fifteen, and was still in short pants, when he first appeared in André Salmon's office at the newspaper *L'Intransigeant,* bringing with him his father's cartoons for publication: "Really a little boy, in short pants, with the lively eye of an adult who is still naive, yet a likely candidate for cruelty; yes a strange gaze shaded by an arch forelock, in a thick wave, like the hard visor of a helmet."[2] Salmon was able to accept some of the boy's own drawings and to give him advice about his poetry. Radiguet could not help being influenced by Apollinaire, perhaps the most imaginative and certainly the best known of the "new" poets. Salmon urged Radiguet to find himself as poet, and to curb his emulation of the typographical experiments of Apollinaire and P.-A. Birot. Lacking time to spend with Radiguet, Salmon then put him in touch with Max Jacob and Jean Cocteau. Thus began an intense literary career of five years' duration, which was cut short by Radiguet's death in December 1923.

It is difficult to assess precisely Jacob's influence on Radiguet, although it seems absolutely certain that this influence was considerable. Extraordinarily original, creative, and paradoxical, Jacob was making a plea for French classicism, order, and clarity, and against Rimbaud and the forces of "disorder" long before Cocteau and Radiguet made this stance their own. His role in the development of the two other writers is far greater than has generally been realized.

Intervening between the first, high hopes of cubism, and the year 1918, in which Radiguet first contacted Salmon and began his career as writer, was of course the enormity of World War I. The formative years for Radiguet's intellectual growth—like those of his contemporaries Malraux (born in 1901) and Sartre (born in 1905)—were precisely those of the war.

With searing lucidity, Sartre and Malraux, each in his own way, understood that the world was not governed by an absolute, immutable truth, that the character of man's role in it belonged to history—war, change, revolution, impermanence, and transitoriness—rather than to destiny and to a divine plan. The destruction wrought by World War I was of a physical order, certainly: economic, social, political, bringing with it the decline of Western Europe. But it also involved the ruin of a mental order, introducing a sense of arbitrariness and the absurd as a permanent mental disposition into our century. It is part of Picasso's brilliance that, even before the war, he had anticipated, in his elaboration of cubism, this loss of a fixed point of view, the loss of the belief in the present as the mere continuation of the past, and the inevitable impossibility of perspective as an adequate filter by means of which to present or view reality in all of its complexity. Later, Malraux would present man as a traveler in a world distinguished by violent upheaval and sudden change, now hoping to control events, now understanding the futility of this, but always unable to escape history's reach as he tries to decipher its meaning. Even on the ocean, as in the first lines of Malraux's *The Conquerors,* man cannot ignore history as it breaks in upon him:

June 25

"A general strike is ordered in Canton."
Since yesterday, this telegraph message has been posted, underlined in red. All the way to the horizon stretches the Indian Ocean, motionless, glassy, lacquered—no telltale wake. The overcast sky weighs down upon

us with a bathhouse atmosphere, surrounds us with the saturated air. Meanwhile the passengers walk with measured tread upon the deck, taking care never to stray too far from the white frame in which will be posted the messages received last night. Each day, the news bulletins specify what drama is beginning; it takes shape; now a direct threat, it haunts every man on the liner. Until now, the hostility of the government of Canton had been displayed in words: now, suddenly, it is acts that the telegrams describe.

While there is no indication that the war introduced death, great grief, or physical suffering into Radiguet's life, it does appear—as was inevitable—to have cast a permanent shadow upon him. In 1918 it was no longer possible to take for granted that belief in the future—or the past—that had seemed so easy before the war began. A firm sense of the immutability of values and institutions had yielded before the terrible awareness of their vulnerability. In Radiguet's case, this awareness appears to have created a sense of spiritual emptiness, a lack of spontaneity, and a disquieting, lucid cynicism. Wise beyond his years, he was described by most of those who knew him as an impressive, cold, observant presence:

All of those who knew Radiguet tell us of a small, near-sighted character, who was generally silent, directing his icy stare amid conversations and laughter. He despised the profession of child prodigy. He refused to be admired for his age. People accused him of being cold-hearted.[3]

In the course of the war, Radiguet witnessed and experienced the removal of many of the restraints that in more normal times contain and hedge around life, giving it rhythm, regularity, and a pattern. By the time he was fifteen years of age, he had already given up his studies at the *lycée* Charlemagne in Paris and was engaged in an affair with a young woman whose husband was at the front; he had even begun to write and was published. His home circumstances appear to have accelerated the process by which he matured at an extraordinary pace. He was the oldest of seven children, and there was no question of his receiving the undivided attention of either parent. His father was some eighteen years older than Radiguet's mother, whom he married when he was thirty-six years old, and most of his energy was absorbed in trying to eke out an existence as a cartoonist/illustrator. His mother, for her part, was fully occupied by the needs of her six younger children. In his relations with his family, there was none of the revolt that characterized Rimbaud's feelings toward his home. Rimbaud did not hesitate to heap invective upon his town, Charleville:

Sir,
You are lucky not to be living in Charleville now. My home-town is the epitome of a stupid provincial town. You can see I have no more illusions about this. Because it is next to Mézières—a town you won't find— because it can see wandering in its streets two or three hundred soldiers, this benighted populace gestures like a curt M. Prudhomme, in a way quite different from the besieged people of Metz and Strasbourg! Retired grocers dressed to the nines in their uniforms are an awful sight![4]

Radiguet claimed that his home—in point of fact no more distinguished than Charleville—was for him an idyllic place: "I did not imagine that any place on earth could surpass in nobility the one in which I was born."[5] And when he started earning money, Radiguet shared some of it with his parents; even after he settled in Paris and became famous, he returned home regularly. But the fact remains that he was only too happy to leave behind him the penurious, lower-middle-class existence of one child among many in an unattractive dormitory suburb of Paris.

Radiguet was not much given to self-confession. By a process of selective memory, he presented only these elements of his early childhood that suited him. Consequently, in his writing there are frequent descriptions of the Marne River and of the Ile-de-France, but virtually no specific details about the real, material circumstances of his own upbringing. One can speculate and perhaps even assume that this suppression of personal detail was grounded in early pain or humiliation. In any case, the small boy in short pants who appeared in André Salmon's office was already endowed with many of the features that would remain as constants in the remaining five and a half years of his life. Salmon, Jacob, and especially Cocteau introduced him to a new world; but Radiguet's basic disposition remained unchanged. His characteristic posture was sphinxlike: that of a terribly lucid, rather cold, judgelike figure looking on, frugal of word, gesture, and facial expression. Of the many portraits and photographs of Radiguet that remain, most present an unsmiling countenance. In complete contrast to Cocteau's volubility and expansiveness, Radiguet spoke very little. It was a rare occasion indeed when he spoke at length; he preferred to observe and listen. In the company of the "Mutual Admiration Society," the group of friends who met on Saturday nights, he might unwind a little, but this was highly unusual: "It is at this very table that one could have heard Radiguet speak for more than five minutes."[6]

As an adolescent living in Saint-Maur, Radiguet had already pushed his experience of life beyond limits that would have hemmed him in in more normal circumstances. In Paris, in the company of Cocteau and others, he experienced the brilliance and the license of the capital to an extraordinary degree. It is an error to believe that, a priori, youth was not encouraged or invited to write and create. On the contrary, with the passing of many of the older literary figures, and the great flux in values brought about by the war, the publishers were on the lookout for new, young talent, and Radiguet's unquestioned gifts were quickly and readily recognized. But, if Radiguet brought to his career in Paris unusual lucidity, great intelligence, and extraordinary maturity, he also brought with him an absence or lack. There was no sign of tenaciously held beliefs, no real spiritual dimension or acknowledgment of transcendent ideals. Instead, the moral "roots" he had were at best very shallow. Religion, for example, plays no part in Radiguet's work. Whereas Cocteau always placed emphasis upon a spiritual element in his writing, and actually returned to the Church for a time, through the intermediary Jacques Maritain, after Radiguet's death, his protégé dismissed religion in a few curt words: "Religion—dead today—and since Jesus—since there are no longer any miracles."[7] His attitude was one of complete skepticism:

> And, to be happy, it appears,
> One must not think of Heaven
> But *I* can think of it without remorse
> When I was born, *it* had died.[8]

The period was of course anything but conducive to deeply rooted beliefs. Gide's *boutade* to Maurice Barrès has rather general validity for the time: "Born in Paris of a father from Uzès and a mother from Normandy, where, Monsieur Barrès, do you expect me to take root? So I have made up my mind to travel."[9] Radiguet's version of "travel" was to make himself extraordinarily available to all that Paris had to offer. This meant, on the one hand, the brilliant companionship of a unique artistic and literary community. But on the other hand it revealed itself as a willingness to follow all the avenues that perversity opened up, without restraint, moderation, or even the instinct for self-preservation.

Initially Radiguet would take the last train from the Bastille station home to Parc Saint-Maur. Increasingly he would miss it, and have either to walk home through the woods of Vincennes or find a bed of fortune in the capital: with the Hugos, in Cocteau's mother's house near the Madeleine, while she was still willing to put him up, in nearby hotels in the rue Lavoisier or the rue de Surène, or in seedy accommodations in Montmartre or Montparnasse. As he came to spend more and more—and most—of his time with Cocteau or his friends, the pace of his life quickened. The underside of a dazzling social life included heavy drinking, liaisons both heterosexual and homosexual, and even the use of opium. He and Cocteau were a source of fascination to their companions:

Cocteau and Radiguet formed a pair of inseparables whom we never grew tired of watching, Georges Auric and I. Mixed in was a trace of diabolical curiosity: we were eager to see how far Radiguet would follow his taste for freedom, how he would manage to free himself from the tutelage of his mentor. We would observe him with women, with alcohol. We came very close to encouraging him. It was a dangerous game. [10]

Unrestrained as he was in his exploration of excess, Radiguet was indeed playing a dangerous game that eventually turned his head, weakened his will to work and ability to concentrate, and, by affecting his health, even contributed to his death. In the final months of his life, there was some indication that Radiguet might have wished to restore some order or direction to his life, or that some order might have been introduced from the outside. Had he lived, he would have been obliged to enter the army; he should have gone in earlier, but the intercession of his publisher Grasset on his behalf had led to the granting of a deferment. In addition, there was some talk, in the final months, of his marrying Bronya Perlmutter. In either situation—or both—he would have been removed from the exhausting irregularity of the dissolute life that had come to be his.

Much of Radiguet's work has about it the character of a quest or search: some sense of a lack of direction, followed by the ardent pursuit of a center. Exposed first of all to the avant-garde, and solicited by it, he wrote poetry that might correctly be called "cubist." But, whereas moral rigor was largely lacking in Radiguet, intellectual or aesthetic rigor was less noticeably absent. More and more, he came to pursue coherence or consistency, some kind of framework or scheme from within which to write. Whereas Cocteau adopted "classicism" with the same facility that he had shown earlier in opting for symbolism, epic patriotism, the New Spirit, cubism, or even dada, Radiguet seems to have taken the return to traditional sources more seriously. He made no distinction among the writers of the Middle Ages, the sixteenth century, or the seventeenth in his understanding of "classicism"—no more than did Charles Maurras, the leader of *Action Française*—but, having elected "classicism" as a model, he tried to bring his own writing and thinking into alignment with it. This involved him in a return to the novel at a time when Breton and his group spurned it, and the adoption of regularly rhymed verse to present traditional themes in a period when the definition of poetry was looser than it had ever been. Apollinaire might find poetry in any number of features of modern life:

> You read the prospectuses the catalogs the posters that sing out loud
> That's this morning's poetry and for prose there are newspapers
> There are serials for 25 centimes full of detective stories
> . . . .
> I saw this morning a pretty street of which I have forgotten the name
> . . . .
> In the morning three times a siren wails there
> A bad-tempered bell barks at about noon
> The lettering on signs and walls
> Billboards and notices shriek like parrots
> I love the grace of this industrial street.[11]

But Radiguet, after initially being tempted by the excitement of the present, turned his back upon it, coming to prefer an aesthetic grounded in a past that preceded even the nineteenth century. Like Maurras and the partisans of *Action Française,* he preferred the *ancien régime* to the Revolution and its various progeny, and his literary or aesthetic preferences were inseparable from his right-wing ideological tastes, although there is no evidence of his expressing any active interest in the return of the monarchy.

It is impossible to know what Radiguet's eventual development would have been had he lived beyond the age of twenty. Jacques

Rivière, using the available evidence of the extant work, asked: "If he had lived, would Radiguet ever have taken his place among the great explorers of the human heart?"[12] His answer was categorical: "Nothing in what he has left us authorizes us to assert this." But, in response to this judgment, Albert Thibaudet reached an opposite conclusion, stating as his opinion that, if Radiguet had lived, "I am convinced of it, [he would have produced] twenty masterpieces and [had] the career of one of the great writers of the twentieth century."[13]

This is just one of a number of questions to which a wholly satisfactory answer cannot be given. In fact, Radiguet is not a writer who lends himself to simple, reductive answers. Little given to the confessional mode, concealing as much as he gives away, a terribly lucid man—or boy—[14]he retains a certain core of mystery that eludes easy or simplistic analysis. And the degree to which his career was intertwined with that of Cocteau, along with Cocteau's determination to erect a myth around his protégé's life, makes it even more difficult to understand him fully.

In the relationship between Cocteau and Radiguet, it is more often than not impossible to know who influenced whom and to what extent. There can be no doubt that the older writer played an enormous part in the elaboration of the younger one's work, finding, for example, a conclusion for *Devil in the Flesh,* and rewriting much of *Count d'Orgel* after Radiguet's death. A parallel reading of the two writers in the period from 1920 until 1923 shows many similarities both in prose and in poetry. In naming just the most obvious features, it is possible to see many points of comparison between, on the one hand, *Thomas l'Imposteur* and *Le Grand Ecart,* and on the other *Devil in the Flesh* and *Count d'Orgel.* Each of the works presents a young man in the throes of "growing up": each is, in other words, a sentimental education. The opening of *Thomas,* like that of *Devil in the Flesh,* makes it clear that the action described could not have taken place in time of peace. In effect, war removes the respective protagonists from customary reality and occasions events that would otherwise be impossible. And the sexual hesitation of Jacques Forestier in *Le Grand Ecart,* explicitly stated, has its parallel, more subtly stated, in François's attachment for the count and his wife in *Count d'Orgel.* Moreover, a juxtaposition of Cocteau's *Poésies 1917–1920* and *Vocabulaire* with Radiguet's poetry from the period reveals an extraordinary number of parallels. When it is recalled that the two collections by Cocteau contain many echoes of his little-known first collections, dating from around 1910, it seems clear that *his* influence on Radiguet's poetry was considerable: much greater than has generally been realized.

Cocteau himself liked to deny his own influence on the younger writer, claiming that Radiguet, after reading the avant-garde writers of the period, including Cocteau himself, then went on to teach *them* a lesson:

At the age of fourteen, Raymond Radiguet knew everything and taught us everything. And we enrolled in his school. . . . it is necessary to point out that Raymond Radiguet had learned his classics. Raymond Radiguet's classics were our books. He would read them at his father's, in the bottom of a boat, on the Marne, in Parc Saint-Maur where he lived. . . .

He appeared on the scene as a contradictor; that is, he would contradict everything that was brand new for us. He was the first to tell me: "You must write like everybody."

What he called "writing like everybody" meant, for example, doing a novel or a poem in verse. . . .

What is more, Apollinaire told me twenty times that *he* tried to write like Anatole France. He did not succeed, fortunately![15]

However convincing Cocteau's remarks, made in 1951, may seem, they are, in fact quite inaccurate. Radiguet was actually almost fifteen when they first met, and their close association did not begin until about two years later. As a youth, moreover, Radiguet was reading the traditional classics of French literature; his classics were not just Jean Cocteau and the latter's contemporaries. This is all the more true since Jean Cocteau had published almost nothing in the way of "avant-garde" pieces at this time. When Radiguet made his debut as a writer, moreover, far from contradicting the new poets, his style was so close to them that Apollinaire took offense, thinking that Radiguet was parodying him! And Cocteau's implied closeness to Apollinaire ("twenty times") is a minor deception that Cocteau was fond of spreading abroad. In reality, Apollinaire did not feel close to Cocteau, and was intensely distrustful of his sincerity. In sum, Cocteau's remarks (or at least their inaccuracy) underline the difficulty of accepting his version of the relationship. It seems perfectly clear that Cocteau's influence on the younger man was far greater than he was, for whatever reason, willing to admit.

On the other hand, it must be conceded that there was about Radiguet a seriousness, a gravity, that had often been lacking in Cocteau. It may well be that Radiguet, a more diligent reader of the major classics of French literature than his friend, helped persuade him to write books that could be placed in the long tradition of French literary history, and not just be intended to dazzle contemporary society friends. Cocteau insisted on his own identity as poet, but never claimed to be a thinker:

> But words are useful to me and I am not an intellectual. I seldom speak to myself or at least I need to speak aloud. I rarely think, I need dialogues. . . . I do not have to contemplate action; I have, quite simply, to act.[16]

Radiguet, much more of a thinker, appears to have convinced Cocteau to stop, take stock, and, for once, think long and rather hard about the kind of works he should write. A first fruit was the critical essay *Le Secret Professionnel*. In the 1920s, moreover, Cocteau's most productive decade, there were many others.

It is a moot point whether Radiguet, for his part, would have had the resolve to continue writing had he been spared. Certainly there are many clues in notes or drafts he left that he did not lack *ideas* for the future. In the year of his death, he entertained the thought of a work on Charles d'Orléans, the fifteenth-century poet, whom he greatly admired. He also contemplated a possible novel laying bare the steps and motives that might lead a man to commit suicide.[17]

> Scene—the unhappy woman that we—her husband and I—get drunk— undress her at her home—mysterious motive of the husband. The fact is that he is in love with me—this mystery which leads one to wish to share, as one does one's fortune.[18]

In *Count d'Orgel,* the reader has no more than a strong impression that the two male characters, François and the count, may be "reaching for" each other in their shared attraction for Mahaut, the countess. In still another of the *Notes Romanesques,* Radiguet's fascination with eccentric sexuality takes the form of the love shared by a father and his son for the same girl. This strategy was of course used much later by Jean Cocteau in his play *Les Parents Terribles,* and its orgins *may perhaps* be traced back to Radiguet's first encountering Alice, the model for Marthe in *Devil in the Flesh,* when she was in the company of his father. There is some suggestion of a possible relationship between Maurice Radiguet and Alice.

Well read, lucid, rather cynical and exploitative, endowed with an extraordinary gift for analysis, Radiguet was a disquieting and gifted presence on the Parisian literary scene. Rejecting the ready-made canon of realism, refusing to find truth in the object, the surface, the material reality, he substituted for it the subject: the person in his hidden motives, depth, contradictions, and complexity. It is a tenet of his art that there is more to the individual than meets the eye. Nearsighted, he was gifted with an exceptional power of "sight": the ability to penetrate below the appearance presented by human behavior to its secret roots. Radiguet himself deserves to be better known, for there is more to him than has been commonly perceived, as man or boy, as novelist, critic, and poet.

Notes and References

Chapter One

1. François Mauriac, "Raymond Radiguet," in *Men I Hold Great,* trans. Elsie Pell (New York: Philosophical Library, 1951), p. 123.

2. Ibid., p. 120.

3. Ibid., p. 123.

4. "Ile-de-France, Ile d'Amour," in *Oeuvres Complètes* ed. Simone Lamblin (Paris, 1959), 2:323–44. *Oeuvres Complètes* hereafter cited as *OC* 1 or *OC* 2. "Ile-de-France, Ile d'Amour" is a long, unfinished panegyric to Radiguet's native province that may have been intended as an appendix to *Devil in the Flesh.* All translations from French or German are by the author unless otherwise stated.

5. "Every Monday morning we could read in the newspapers reports of fights that broke out the day before in one of those Nogent taverns by the Marne." "Ile-de-France, Ile d'Amour," *OC,* 2:325.

6. Ibid., pp. 326–27. La Varenne is south of St.-Maur, whereas Nogent-sur-Marne is to the north.

7. "At the Champigny train station, where all the military trains went by, the strategic center for patriotism. . . . At the start of the war my whole being was physically more shaken than by the first pangs of love. If that is patriotism, then I felt patriotic." Ibid., p. 334.

8. In early 1915, Jean Cocteau was reciting his long poem "Hymne au général Joffre" in the salons of Paris. It was published on the front page of *Figaro,* February 14, 1915, to Cocteau's delight. Jean-Jacques Kihm, Elizabeth Sprigge, Henri C. Behar, *Jean Cocteau, l'homme et les miroirs* (Paris: Editions de la table ronde, 1968), pp. 85–86.

9. Maurice Radiguet and Marcel Arnac, *Kolossâle Kollection* (Paris: Ollendorf, 1915). The title may be derived from one of the stories, involving a M. Topinangrad. He is dejected at being surrounded by objects made in Germany. He undresses to make love to a Flemish streetwalker. Upon her exclaiming, "Kolossâl!" he remembers that even he had been "made in Germany." His parents spent their honeymoon in Bavaria.

10. Francis Poulenc, letter of September 11, 1924, *Correspondance,* cited by Kihm, *Jean Cocteau,* p. 156.

11. Undated letter in Keith Goesch, *Raymond Radiguet: étude biographique* (Paris, Geneva, 1955), p. 2.

12. "Ne nous étonnons plus si votre force fine / Ajoute au laurier noir les roses de l'amour, / Car vous mêlez en vous le sang de Joséphine /

A celui de la Pompadour." Jean Cocteau, undated poem to Raymond Radiguet, cited in Kihm, *Jean Cocteau,* p. 143.

13. In Goesch, *Raymond Radiguet,* p. 24.

14. Undated letter to his parents, in Liliana Garuti delli Ponti, ed., *Gli Inediti* (Unpublished works) (Parma, 1967), p. 206.

15. Jean-Honoré Fragonard, *L'Escarpolette* (The swing) Wallace Collection, London. Radiguet's preference for the small subject over the large, and his penchant for parks, mythological motifs emptied of sublime content, eroticism, and especially love-making in a rustic setting are features that allow his work to be compared with that of rococo artists of the eighteenth century.

16. In "Le Vieux Saltimbanque" (The old clown), a prose-poem in *Le Spleen de Paris* (Parisian spleen), Charles Baudelaire detects a tragic dimension in a fairground scene of apparent gaiety. He calls the occasion a "solemnity." "C'était une de ces solennités" ("It was one of these solemnities"). *Oeuvres Complètes* (Paris: Gallimard, 1961), p. 247.

17. Camille Aymard, in *La Touraine Républicaine,* July 19, 1924, cited by Goesch, *Raymond Radiguet,* p. 24.

18. Jean Cocteau, "Avant-propos" (Preface) to Goesch, *Raymond Radiguet,* p. ix.

19. Arthur Rimbaud, "Les Premières Communions," "Les Poètes de sept ans," in *Oeuvres Complètes* (Paris: Gallimard, 1972), pp. 60, 43.

20. One of the first sections of Rimbaud's long poem "Une Saison en enfer" ("A Season in Hell") is entitled "Mauvais Sang" ("Bad Blood"). *Oeuvres Complètes,* p. 94.

21. Roger Nimier, *Journées de lecture* (Days of reading) (Paris: Gallimard, 1965), p. 235.

22. "Souvenirs d'enfance" (Memories of childhood), *OC,* 2:403. These two pages of fragmentary memories are found, along with ten other brief, unfinished drafts, in a section entitled "Désordre" (Disorder) by Simone Lamblin, the editor of *OC. OC,* 2:371–403. "Souvenirs d'enfance" is one of the very few occasions when Radiguet makes mention of specific features of his childhood, such as street names, hats, balloons, shops, etc.

23. Maurice Martin du Gard, "Raymond Radiguet," *Les Nouvelles Littéraires,* September 6, 1924, p. 1.

24. Paul Morand, *"Le Diable* sans confession" *(The Devil* without confession), *Les Nouvelles Littéraires,* January 31, 1963, p. 1.

25. J. R. Bloch, *Carnaval est mort* (The carnival is dead) (Paris: N.R.F., 1920), p. 16.

26. Henry de Montherlant, in a conversation with Maurice Martin du Gard. Maurice Martin du Gard, *Les Mémorables* (Paris: Flammarion, 1957), 1:148.

27. André Salmon, *Souvenirs sans fin, Troisième Epoque, 1920–1940* (Memories without end, third period, 1920–1940) (Paris: Gallimard, 1961), p. 44.

28. Ibid., p. 42.

29. Bernard Faÿ, *Les Précieux* (Paris: Librairie Académique Perrin, 1966), pp. 273–74.

30. Kihm, in *Jean Cocteau*, p. 118, recounts that Max Jacob was eager to present Radiguet to Apollinaire. The latter, distrustful of the younger man, refused.

31. P.-A. Birot, "André Derain," *Sic* 11 (November 1916): unnumbered page.

32. P.-A. Birot, "Poème à crier et à danser: L'AVION" (Poem to be shouted and danced: THE AIRPLANE), *Sic* 23 (November 1917).

33. Jean Cocteau was self-appointed impresario to the six composers, who came to be known as "le Groupe des Six." Georges Auric, Louis Durey, Arthur Honegger, Darius Milhaud, Francis Poulenc, and Germaine Taillefer had little in common beyond varying degrees of friendship for Cocteau, and of musical respect for Erik Satie (1866–1925).

34. Max Jacob, cited by Maurice Martin du Gard, *Les Mémorables*, p. 106.

35. Max Jacob, letter of February 5, 1919, to Raymond Radiguet, *Correspondence, Quimper-Paris, 1876–1921*, ed. François Garnier (Paris: Editions de Paris, 1953), 1:183.

36. Salmon, *Souvenirs sans fin*, p. 45. The reference to Père-Lachaise is a reminder that Radiguet would be buried there, and that Rastignac, a protagonist of Balzac's *Père Goriot*, surveys Paris from the heights of the graveyard at the end of the novel.

37. Ibid.

38. Nadia Odouard, *Les Années Folles de Raymond Radiguet* (The wild years of Raymond Radiguet) (Paris, 1973), pp. 44–54, surveys Radiguet's relations with Marthe and Gaston, drawing upon an article in *Paris-Match*, December 25, 1958: "Dans l'héroïne du *Diable au corps* un homme a reconnu sa femme" (In *Devil in the Flesh* a man recognized his wife).

39. Jean Cocteau, *Le Coq et l'arlequin* (The rooster and the harlequin), in *Rappel à l'ordre* (A call back to order) (Paris: Stock, 1926), p. 28.

40. André Gide, "Lettre ouverte à Jean Cocteau" (Open letter to Jean Cocteau), *Nouvelle Revue Française* 69 (June 1, 1919):127: "I have often said this to you: each time I talk with you, I am reminded of the dialogue between the bear and the squirrel. Whereas I lumber along, you leap about. . . . I reproach you with sacrificing your most charming and brilliant qualities in favor of other more weighty ones which, perhaps, you do not possess."

41. Jean Cocteau, *Le Prince Frivole* (The frivolous prince) (Paris: Mercure de France, 1910). The title piece sets the tone of wan melancholy: "Dédaigneux, frivole et mince, / Rêvasseur et puéril, / J'étais né pour être prince, / Un petit prince en exil" ("Disdainful, frivolous and slim, / A puerile day-dreamer, / I was born to be a prince, / A little prince in exile").

42. Jean Cocteau, "Hymne au général Joffre," cited by Kihm, *Jean Cocteau,* p. 86.

43. André Breton, letter of December 26, 1919, to Tristan Tzara, cited in Kihm, *Jean Cocteau,* p. 112.

44. Marcel Proust, undated letter of 1908 to Jean Cocteau: ". . . I have on occasion thought of you and formulated, with that pointless indiscretion of friends and philosophers, useless wishes; for example that some event might isolate you and wean you from the pleasures of wit, leaving you the time, after sufficient fasting, to develop a true hunger for these fine books, fine paintings, fine countries that you leaf through today with but little appetite. . . ." *Cahiers Jean Cocteau* 1 (1969):17.

45. Maurice Martin du Gard, "Raymond Radiguet," *Les Nouvelles Littéraires,* September 6, 1924, p. 1.

46. Jean Cocteau has often been compared to a tightrope walker, picking a path between positions. Nowhere is his equilibrium more precarious than in "defining" his relations with dada: "The articles that call me a dadaist amuse me greatly, because I am the very type of antidadaist. The dadaists know it well and, if they sometimes ask for my collaboration, it is to prove that their system is to have no system. . . . I invented the extreme right. . . . I feel so far from the left and the right, so close to the extreme left closing the circle with me that they and I are often confused." *Le Coq,* May 1920, unnumbered page.

47. Darius Milhaud, *Notes Without Music* (New York: Knopf, 1953), pp. 98–99.

48. Ibid., p. 99.

49. *Les Pélican* (1921). *OC,* 1:284.

50. The first issue of *Le Coq* (The rooster) was dated May 1920. The following issues were dated June, July/August/September, and November, respectively. The last two issues added the adjective "Parisien" to the title. After November 1920, François Bernouard could no longer see his way to underwriting it.

51. Jean Cocteau, "Dernières Nouvelles" (Latest News), *Le Coq,* May 1920.

52. Jean Cocteau and Raymond Radiguet, *Paul et Virginie,* in Garuti, *Gli Inediti,* pp. 58–159, with facing page translation in Italian. In a letter to his mother (September 1920) Cocteau revealed his sense that he had conceived of something new in the third act: ". . . I have imagined for

the final act a thing that I find very beautiful." *Album Cocteau,* ed. Pierre Chanel (Paris: Tchou, 1970).

53. André Breton, *Premier Manifeste du Surrealisme* (First manifesto of surrealism) (1924): "Surrealism does not allow those who become addicted to it to give it up when they see fit to do so. Everything leads me to believe that it acts upon the mind like drugs; like them it creates a certain state of dependency and can push man into terrible revolts." *Poésie et autre* (Poetry et cetera) (Paris: Club du meilleur livre, 1960), p. 50. Jean Cocteau's description of the effects of poetry in *Le Secret Professionnel* (1922) is comparable: "Poetry in its raw state makes its practitioner live with nausea. This moral nausea comes from death. . . . Poetry, like a drug, continues to act, but turns against the sick poet, and plagues him with misfortune." *Le Secret Professionnel,* in *Poésie Critique* (Critical poetry) (Paris: Gallimard, 1959), pp. 53–54.

54. Jean Cocteau, *Dessins* (Drawings) (Paris: Stock, 1923). *Le Grand Ecart* (The splits) (Paris: Stock, 1923). The title refers both to skating— one fateful scene takes place in a skating rink—and to a wide gap or breach. At the end of the novel, the hero, Jacques Forestier, finds himself cut off from his mother, from the girl he loves, and from society at large. *Thomas l'imposteur* (Thomas the impostor) (Paris: Gallimard, 1923) describes the adventures of a boy who, under an assumed identity, joins the soldiers at the front in World War I. Like the narrator of *Devil in the Flesh,* his adventures are made possible by the extraordinary suspension of normal reality in the war. *Plain-Chant* (Plain-song) (Paris: Stock, 1923) is a long love poem inspired by Cocteau's love for Radiguet. Its regular verse, theme, and title mark Cocteau's return to tradition under Radiguet's influence. *Antigone,* first staged in 1922, was published later (Paris: Gallimard, 1928).

55. Benjamin Péret, untitled article, *Littérature,* October 1922, cited by Kihm, *Jean Cocteau,* p. 144.

56. Jean Cocteau, *Le Grand Ecart,* pp. 18–19.

57. Francis Picabia, "The Cacodylate Eye." The title refers to the treatment of an eye ailment suffered by Picabia with cacodylate.

58. Francis Steegmuller, *Cocteau: A Biography* (Boston, 1970), recounts the incident, p. 308.

59. Ibid.

60. In an interview conducted by the author in Roquebrune, 1970.

61. "Je vous envoie ce mot. Je vous aime tous deux. / J'erre dans le désert . . . Je songe avec effroi / A nos coeurs sourds, muets, aveugles, amoureux. / Je sais que chacun aime—et je pleure tous trois." Beatrice Hastings, untitled poem (November 1921) in Odouard, *Les Années Folles de Raymond Radiguet,* p. 300.

62. Beatrice Hastings, undated letter to Raymond Radiguet, in Odouard, *Les Années Folles de Raymond Radiguet,* p. 279.

63. Raymond Radiguet to the composer Georges Auric, in Steegmuller, *Cocteau,* p. 314.

64. The record of Radiguet's work, in terms of sales and publication information, has been comprehensively covered by Gabriel Boillat, *Un Maître de 17 ans, Raymond Radiguet* (A seventeen-year-old master, Raymond Radiguet) (Neuchâtel, 1973).

65. Jean Cocteau, *D'Un Ordre considéré comme une anarchie* (Of an order considered as an anarchy), in *Poésie Critique* 1:76, 81.

66. Max Jacob, letter of February 5, 1919, *Correspondance,* 1:183.

67. Bernard Grasset, letter of July 12, 1924, to Henri Béraud, in Boillat, *Un Maître de 17 ans, Raymond Radiguet,* p. 27.

68. R. Eglem, untitled article, *Revue des auteurs et des livres* (Review of authors and books), April 20, 1923, in Odouard, *Les Années Folles de Raymond Radiguet,* p. 44.

69. "Jean Cocteau in a rhapsody of affection . . . was taking Radiguet here and there, introducing him to countries, people, pleasures, foods, drinks, failing to understand that he was going too quickly, that this boy, fresh from poverty, could not lead this bohemian, itinerant existence with impunity." Bernard Faÿ, *Les Précieux,* p. 276.

70. Steegmuller, *Cocteau,* p. 308.

71. Jean Hugo, "Pages de journal," *Cahiers Jean Cocteau* 4 (1973):16–17.

72. Ibid., p. 25.

73. Steegmuller, *Cocteau,* p. 314.

74. Cocteau, "Avant-propos," *Count d'Orgel,* in *OC,* 2:10.

Chapter Two

1. Raymond Radiguet to Jacques Doucet, manuscript letter (December 22, 1919), Jacques Doucet Library, Paris.

2. *Jeux Innocents* (1926). No indication of publisher or page numbers. Of these fifteen pieces, eight are also featured elsewhere in Radiguet's *oeuvre.* The seven that remain—"Samedi" (Saturday), "Les Coups de soleil" (Sunstrokes), "Pigeon vole" (Pigeon fly), "L'Autre Bouche" (The other mouth), "La Créole" (The Creole girl), "Bains publics" (Public baths), and "Jeux Innocents" (Innocent games)—are all short and share with *Le Joues en feu* the themes of love making in a rustic setting and the loss of virginity. *OC,* 1:147–55. Unless otherwise indicated, all of Radiguet's poems discussed here are found in *Oeuvres Complètes,* Vol. 1, ed. Simone Lamblin (Paris, 1959). Cited as *OC* 1.

3. Garuti, ed., *Gli Inediti,* with facing page translation in Italian, pp. 161–90.

4. Jean Cocteau, preface to *La Règle du jeu* (The rule of the game), *OC,* 2:279. This manuscript, a fragmentary journal of critical comments, was not published until 1957 (Monaco: Editions du Rocher).

5. Jean Cocteau, *Entretiens avec André Fraigneau* (Interviews with André Fraigneau) (Paris: Bibliothèque 10/18, 1965), pp. 35–36, provides one of many examples of his considering Radiguet to be comparable to Rimbaud: "At fourteen, Raymond Radiguet knew everything and taught us everything. . . . He is the prodigy of the novel as Rimbaud is the prodigy of poetry."

6. Arthur Rimbaud, "A la Musique," in *Oeuvres Complètes* (Paris: Gallimard, 1972), pp. 21–22.

7. Ibid., p. 251. Letter to Paul Demeny (Charleville, May 15, 1871).

8. While in England with Radiguet, Cocteau had a dream about walking sticks, which he related to his host, Reginald Bridgeman. It is rather illustrative of the difference between the two friends that Bridgeman should comment: "Radiguet would have been inclined to pooh-pooh the reality of dreams, but Jean believed in them and knew how to poetize them." Steegmuller, *Cocteau,* pp. 303–4.

9. P.-A. Birot, "Gino Severini, Première Exposition Futuriste" (Gino Severini, first futurist exhibition), *Sic* 2 (February 1916):no page number.

10. "Sounds Ideas Colors Shapes."

11. Louise Faure-Favier, "A Guillaume Apollinaire, mon ami" (To Guillaume Apollinaire, my friend), *Sic* 37/38/39 (one combined issue) (January and February 15, 1919).

12. "Poème," *OC,* 1:111

13. Daniel-Henry Kahnweiler, *Juan Gris, His Life and Work,* trans. Douglas Cooper (New York: H. N. Abrams, 1969), p. 14.

14. Raymond Radiguet to Tristan Tzara, manuscript letter (May 15, 1919): "In Paris, your arrival is announced. For when?" Jean Cocteau to Tzara, manuscript letter (June 1, 1919): "I should like to know you, speak with you about your poems, which touch me." Tzara was of course still in Zurich at this time. Both letters in Jacques Doucet Library, Paris.

15. In *Le Coq et l'arlequin,* Cocteau prefers the French rooster to the Italian or foreign harlequin. In *Le Coq,* the journal that Cocteau edited in 1920, he again takes up position for French art against foreign—in this instance American—influences.

16. Radiguet, in the style of Max Jacob, appears to be making a pun on the words *divers prénoms* ("various first names"), which may be heard as *d'hiver prénoms* ("first names of winter").

17. "Couleurs sans danger" (Harmless colors), the first poem of *Le Bonnet d'âne. OC,* 1:129.

18. Gerald Kamber, *Max Jacob and the Poetics of Cubism* (Baltimore: Johns Hopkins, 1971), stresses the primacy, in Jacob's poetry and in cubist painting, of the artistic reality created over everyday reality, and the attempt to make the reader concentrate exclusively on the work itself ("Cubism and Painting," pp. 20–30).

19. Jean Cocteau, "Températures," in *Poésies, 1917–1920* (Paris, Editions de la Sirène, 1920), p. 78.

20. Guillaume Apollinaire, "Merveilles de la guerre," in *Calligrammes* (1918). *Oeuvres Poétiques* (Paris: Gallimard, 1956), p. 271.

21. "Prise d'armes," in *OC*, 1:139. Rousseau had in fact been dead for some nine years at this time. But the visual images of bright colors and of Rousseau with a paintbrush in his hand do indeed recall several works by this painter, including his *Self-Portrait* (1890).

22. In his *Le Prince Frivole* (1910), Cocteau had frequent recourse to the rondel.

23. In the first *Joues en feu*, "Pelouse" (Lawn) makes a comparison between the girl's memories of childhood and a lawn: "Pelouse de votre enfance / A peine plus haut que le gazon" ("Lawn of your childhood / Scarcely higher than the turf"). *OC*, 1:91–92.

24. Evariste Désiré de Forges de Parny, "Au Gazon foulé par Eléonore," in *Elégies, Livre III. Oeuvres* (Paris: Garnier, n.d.), p. 75: "De notre amoureux badinage / Ne gardez point le témoignage: / Vous me feriez trop de jaloux."

25. Again and again in *Poésies 1917–1920*, Cocteau associates the image of red cheeks with that of a rose and its petals: "Romance," p. 55; "Locutions" (Sayings), p. 57; "Sobre las olas," p. 69.

26. Foreword to *Les Joues en feu*. *OC*, 1:16.

27. Steegmuller, *Cocteau*, p. 271.

28. Thanks to the poet Ann Deagon, who first saw the connection with the traditional tale when this poem was described to her.

29. No pun intended.

30. Stéphane Mallarmé, "Brise Marine," in *Poésie. Oeuvres Complètes* (Paris: Gallimard, 1945), p. 38.

31. "Ebauches," in *Vers Libres* (Free verse). *Gli Inediti*, ed. Garuti, p. 188.

32. "Vénus Démasquee" (Venus Unmasked), in *OC*, 1:50.

33. "L'Etoile de Venus" (The Star of Venus), in *OC*, 1:56.

34. Jean Cocteau, *Le Discours du grand sommeil* (Paris: Gallimard, 1925; reprint, 1967), p. 164.

35. Jean Cocteau, "La Mort d'un cygne," in *Vocabulaire*, p. 57.

36. The two poems in Gide's *Anthologie de la poésie française* (Paris: Gallimard, 1949) are "Amélie," from *Devoirs de vacances,* and "Avec la

mort tu te maries" (With death you are wed), from *Les Joues en feu,* pp. 773, 774.

37. David Noakes, *Raymond Radiguet* (Paris, 1952; reprint, 1968), p. 16.

38. "Pêcheur pris dans ses propres filets / Pris dans les filets qu'il tendit" ("Fisherman caught in his own nets / Caught in the nets that he cast"). Raymond Radiguet, untitled poem in Odouard, *Les Années Folles de Raymond Radiguet,* unnumbered page of appendix. A comparable image occurs in "Le Promenoir des Deux Amants" by Tristan: "Vois mille Amours qui se vont prendre / Dans les filets de tes cheveux" ("See a thousand Loves that are caught / In the nets of your hair"). Tristan l'Hermite, *Choix de pages* (Paris: Rougerie, 1960), ed. Amédée Carriat, p. 40. Parny is another probable influence. His poem "A Eléonore," in *Mélanges, Oeuvres de Parny,* begins: "Aimer à treize ans" ("To be in love at thirteen"), p. 334. Radiguet has a short piece in *Joues en feu* entitled "Les Fiancés de treize ans" (The thirteen-year-old fiancés). *OC,* 1:126.

39. Jean Cocteau, "Seine et Oise," in *Le Prince Frivole,* p. 37.

40. Jean Cocteau, "Le Problème" (The problem), in *La Lampe d'Aladin* (Aladdin's lamp) (Paris: De Bouville, 1909), unnumbered page.

41. "Sur la mort d'une rose" (On the death of a rose), in Odouard, *Les Années Folles de Raymond Radiguet,* unnumbered page.

Chapter Three

1. François Mauriac, "Radiguet," *Cahiers de la quinzaine,* 13th cahier, 18th series (1927). Mauriac praises Radiguet for understanding intuitively that his was a period of uncertainty and transition, pp. 107–28.

2. André Breton, "First Manifesto of Surrealism," in *Manifestoes of Surrealism* (Ann Arbor: University of Michigan Press, 1972), pp. 14–15.

3. Fernand Vandérem, "Les Lettres et la vie," *La Revue de Paris,* September–October 1920, p. 430.

4. Pierre Reverdy, *Self-Defence,* in *Nord-Sud, Self-Defence et autres écrits sur l'art et la poésie, 1917–1926* (Nord-Sud, self-defense and other writings on art and poetry, 1917–1926) (Paris: Flammarion, 1975), pp. 111, 119.

5. This postwar situation is clearly described in Theodore Zeldin, "Gerontocracy," in *France 1848–1945* (Oxford: Oxford University Press, 1977), 2:1083–1120.

6. Fernand Vandérem, "Les Lettres et la vie," *La Revue de Paris,* May-June 1920. p. 186.

7. *Littérature* itself stopped appearing in 1922.

8. Roland Dorgelès, *Les Croix de bois* (Paris: Albin Michel, 1919; reprint, 1931), p. 290.

9. Roland Dorgelès, letter of July 2, 1923, to Raymond Radiguet, cited in Goesch, *Raymond Radiguet,* p. 45.

10. *Le Diable au corps,* in *OC,* 1:289, will hereafter be cited as *D,* references to *OC* 1.

11. Jean Cocteau, letter of December 16, 1923, to Daniel Halévy, cited in Boillat, *Un Maître de 17 ans,* p. 39.

12. Max Jacob, letter of July 12, 1923, to Jouhandeau. *Correspondance,* 2:182.

13. Bernard Grasset, letter of March 3, 1923, cited by Boillat, *Un Maître de 17 ans,* p. 32.

14. Ibid., pp. 33–34.

15. Bernard Faÿ, *Les Précieux,* p. 58.

16. Max Jacob, letter to Jean Cocteau, January 30, 1923. *Correspondance,* 2:142.

17. Boillat, *Un Maître de 17 ans,* gives a comprehensive view of the novel's reception by the critics, pp. 41–42.

18. "Mon Premier. Roman, *Le Diable au corps"* (My first novel, *Devil in the Flesh*), *OC,* 2:249–51.

19. Shakespeare, *Macbeth,* act 1, sc. 3, in *Complete Works* (Oxford: Oxford University Press, 1957), p. 847. These words are spoken by all the witches immediately before the arrival of Macbeth and Banquo.

20. Henry James, preface to *The American* (New York: Charles Scribner, 1935), p. xvii.

21. These features of the romance are enumerated by John B. Stevens, *Medieval Romance: Themes and Approaches* (New York: Norton, 1974), p. 34.

22. To the obvious Freudian imagery (the key, the lock . . .) one mght add other images in this scene recalling a traditional rite of passage. The youth leaves the food provided by his mother as he goes to another woman; he comes to a guarded bridge over a river at night, etc.

23. These events and settings (gardens, alcoves, etc.) are treated by Moshe Lazar, "Le Jardin et l'alcôve," in *Amour Courtois et fin' amors* (Courtly love and fin' amors) (Paris: Klincksieck, 1964), pp. 123–27.

24. Gottfried von Strassburg, *Tristan und Isolde* (Darmstadt: Wissenschaftliche Buchgesellschaft, 1967), ed. Friedrich Ranke, pp. 16, 733 ff.

25. Ibid., pp. 16, 689 ff.

26. Shakespeare, *Romeo and Juliet,* act 5, sc. 3, in *Complete Works,* p. 794. Escalus, the Prince of Verona, addresses Capulet in the final scene of the play.

Chapter Four

1. Paul Valéry, letter (April 8, 1923) to Raymond Radiguet, cited in Goesch, *Raymond Radiguet*, p. 49.

2. *Ball at Count d'Orgel's*, trans. Malcolm Cowley (New York, 1929); *Count d'Orgel*, trans. Alan Sheridan Smith (London: Calder & Boyars, 1969). *Le Bal du comte d'Orgel* will hereafter be cited as *B*, with page references to vol. 2 of the *Oeuvres Complètes* (*OC*).

3. *D*, *OC*, 1:457. These are the last words of the novel.

4. Jean Cocteau, *Le Grand Ecart* (Paris: Stock, 1923); *Thomas l'imposteur* (Paris: Gallimard, 1923); *Plain-Chant* (Paris: Stock, 1923); *Antigone* (Paris: Gallimard, staged 1922, published 1928).

5. Jean Cocteau, letters to his mother, from July 1922 on, cited by Andrew Oliver, "Cocteau, Radiguet et la genèse du *Bal du comte d'Orgel*," *Cahiers Jean Cocteau* 4 (1973):41–69. He used equally laudatory terms in a letter to Max Jacob: "Radiguet is completing his new novel. Truly miraculous." In Max Jacob, letter of October 18, 1922, *Correspondance*, 2:128.

6. Oliver, "Cocteau, Radiguet," p. 45. Oliver offers convincing evidence that Cocteau played a far greater role in the composition of *B* than had been realized.

7. "Début d'un journal," *OC*, 2:397.

8. Jean Cocteau, foreword to *B*, *OC*, 2:11

9. Eugène Montfort, in *Les Marges*, July 1924, cited by Andrew Oliver, "Cocteau, Radiguet," p. 55: "All that we can say about *Count d'Orgel* by the late Raymond Radiguet is that it is very good Cocteau, which justifies the reservations of M. Jacques Rivière, and the enthusiasm of the publisher Grasset."

10. The car breaks down and a crowd forms around it, commenting on the affluent passengers. *B*, 35.

11. Jean Cocteau, *Le Grand Ecart* (1923), p. 166: "Jacques felt his mood grow somber again. He knew that to love on earth one must abide by its customs and his heart was no longer in it."

12. Steegmuller, *Cocteau*, p. 139.

13. Mahaut's voice is deep and masculine, while Anne's is a falsetto. It would be plausible to see in Anne an attraction to François, and vice-versa. From such a (depth psychology) point of view, Mahaut is merely the "go-between" for the two men.

14. Just as François's last name—de Séryeuse—is feminine in gender.

15. The name "Robin" has the added advantage in French of suggesting, since the Middle Ages, a conventional character: the scheming peasant—very appropriate for Paul. Another character, Prince Mirza, was

undoubtedly inspired by Prince Firouz of Persia, a friend of Cocteau's and Radiguet's, whom Cocteau called "Prince Turquoise."

16. Jacques Rivière, in a note accompanying publication of an excerpt from *B, Nouvelle Revue Française*, June 1924, p. 693.

17. Albert Thibaudet, "Réflêxions sur la littérature," *N.R.F.*, July 1924, p. 197.

18. André Gide, *Journal, 1889–1939* (Paris: Gallimard, 1951), pp. 1149–50.

19. "Ile-de-France, Ile d'Amour," *OC*, 2:338: "Did not an eminent writer, a member of the French Academy, seriously reproach me with failing to tell the color of my heroine's eyes? What about Mme de Clèves? What color were her eyes?"

20. Radiguet's treatment of objects, nonutilitarian, a source of mystery, is intriguingly close to that practiced by the surrealists. For example, André Breton in *Nadja* (Paris: Gallimard, rpt. 1928), p. 63: ". . . I had gone to the flea-market of St. Ouen (I am often there, in search of these objects that you find nowhere else, out of fashion, in pieces, unusable, almost incomprehensible, perverse, at least in the sense I understand)."

21. Mme de Lafayette, *La Princesse de Clèves* (Geneva: Droz, 1950), pp. 35–36.

22. Cocteau, *Le Grand Ecart*, p. 19.

23. The expression "Dance to the Music of Time" is of course taken from the title of the painting by Poussin. The title is also used by the writer Anthony Powell for his series of novels (Boston: Little, Brown, 1975).

24. Boillat, *Un Maître de 17 ans*, p. 83.

25. Anne is described as a man who resembled his ancestors, and "for whom, Versailles and two or three comparable places, nature is a virgin forest, where a man of breeding 'does not venture.' " There is a gap of misunderstanding between husband and wife: "The difference between Anne and Mahaut was deep. It was that which, over the centuries, opposed the Grimoard to the Orgel like day to night—that antagonism of court nobility and feudal nobility." *B*, 63.

26. Rastignac and Vautrin (of Balzac's *Human Comedy*) and Julien Sorel (of Stendhal's *The Red and the Black*) are of course all intent on obtaining fame and fortune.

27. To quote just a few examples: Paul Robin eventually has an affair with Hester Wayne, and the news of this liaison ruins another, much more serious affair he has conducted with a married woman. Mme Forbach, with whom François stays, had been a widow for thirty years, while his mother had been left a widow very young. Stretching the reader's credulity, Radiguet even makes of Prince Mirza's niece a widow; she is all of fifteen! *B*, 111.

28. André Malraux, *Les Conquérants,* in *Romans* (Paris: Gallimard, 1947), p. 9. These are the first words of the novel.

29. Charles Maurras, *Mes Idées Politiques* (My political ideas) (Paris: Fayard, 1968), p. 113. The year 1968 marked the one hundredth anniversary of Maurras's birth and saw the publication of a number of anthologies of his writings, including this one.

30. Charles Maurras, *Critique et Poésie* (Criticism and Poetry) (Paris: Librairie académique Perrin, 1968), p. 189: "it devoured Chénier, that Revolutionary Beast. . . ."

31. Maurras, *Mes Idées Politiques,* p. 114.

32. Ernst Nolte, *Three Faces of Fascism* (New York: Holt, Rinehart, & Winston 1966), p. 60, gives one example among many of Maurras's xenophobia: "During the very first days of his stay in Paris, he [Maurras] was 'struck, moved, almost hurt,' to come across so many foreign names on the boulevards, names which were distinguished by the abhorrent letters 'K' or 'W' or 'Z.' " Maurras expressed his contempt for Americans, a "nebulous aggregate of population," p. 130.

33. "Notes Critiques Diverses," *OC,* 2:382–83.

Chapter Five

1. Marcel Arland, *Une Epoque* (Paris: Corrêa, 1930), p. 53.

2. Ibid.

3. Fernand Vandérem, "Les Lettres et la vie," *Revue de Paris,* August 15, 1920, p. 854, reviews the works by Chadourne and Obey. Like most of the critics of the period, Vandérem is deeply aware that his period is a time of change, crisis, and searching.

4. For Charles Maurras, the French Revolution created an absolute divide. Before it, France was a divine entity. The revolution brought dissolution: "When Maurras speaks of the *Déesse France,* he is thinking of the 'most perfect society' Europe has ever known, the society of the *ancien régime* and of the 'first city of the world,' the Paris of the eighteenth century . . . under the monarchy *ordre et progrès* . . . under the republic *désordre et diminution.* . . ." Nolte, *Three Faces of Fascism,* evoking Maurras's *Enquête sur la monarchie* (Inquiry into the monarchy), p. 105.

5. Fernand Vandérem, "Les Lettres et la vie," *Revue de Paris,* May-June 1920, p. 186.

6. "Notes secrètes sur quelques poètes cubistes" (Secret notes on a few cubist poets), *OC,* 2:274–75. Unless otherwise stated, references are to *OC* 2, in which most of Radiguet's critical essays are found. Most of the articles that appeared in Radiguet's lifetime are short (2–3 pp.) reviews, often of Cocteau's works from the period. Most of the posthumous publications are equally short. A number of them, fragmentary and unfinished, are gathered into a section entitled *"Desordre"* (Disorder) by Simone Lam-

blin, the editor of *OC* (pp. 307–403). Two longer essays are "Règle du jeu" (Rule of the game), *OC*, 2:277–316, a series of reflections on literature, and "Ile-de-France, Ile d'Amour," a panegyric to Radiguet's native province, *OC*, 2:323–44.

7. Max Jacob, letter of June 10, 1921, to Jean Cocteau, *Correspondance*, 1:229.

8. Ibid., to Kahnweiler, end of June 1921, 2:18.

9. Max Jacob, "Roman Feuilleton" (Series novel), in *Le Cornet à dés* (The dice box), is one of many prose poems by Jacob written to experiment with Parisian "street" language or situation Radiguet's "Galanterie Française" (French gallantry), *OC*, 2:199–201, is a similar, lighthearted piece, set in a crowded subway car.

10. Max Jacob, letter to Jacques Doucet, January 11, 1917, *Correspondance*, 1:120.

11. Ibid., p. 134.

12. Ibid., February 21, 1917, p. 139.

13. Philippe Soupault, letter to Tristan Tzara, January 28, 1919, cited by Noakes, *Raymond Radiguet*, p. 38.

14. Letter to André Breton, August 19, 1919, cited by Noakes, *Raymond Radiguet*, p. 39.

15. *Littérature* 9 (November 1919):1.

16. "Reply to the Inquiry: Why Do You Write?", *Littérature* 12 (February 1920):*OC*, 2:204.

17. Tristan Tzara, "Open Letter to Jacques Rivière," *Littérature* 10 (December 1919):3.

18. Benjamin Péret, "Carte Blanche," *Littérature* 16 (September–October 1920):40.

19. Tristan Tzara, "Chronique: pour faire un poème dadaïste" (Chronicle: to make a dadaist poem), *Littérature* 15 (July–August 1920):18.

20. Péret, "Carte Blanche," p. 40.

21. Louis Aragon, "Ouverture de la grande saison Dada" (Opening of the big dada season), *Littérature* 19 (May 1921):16–17.

22. Fernand Vandérem, "Les Lettres et la vie," *Revue de Paris*, September–October 1920, p. 428.

23. Ibid., p. 431.

24. "Jean Cocteau," *OC*, 2:258 (December 1919). This article was first written for Jacques Doucet and was published in *OC* 2 for the first time.

25. "Dada ou le cabaret du néant" (Dada or the nothingness bar), *OC*, 2:271–72. Dated May 1920, this manuscript, belonging to André Breton, was published in 1956 for the first time.

26. "Dada ou le cabaret du néant." The title is presumably borrowed from the poem "Spleen" by Léon-Paul Fargue. This concludes: "Dans ce

cabaret du néant / Qu'est-ce que notre vie?" ("In this nothingness bar / What is life?").

27. "La Règle du jeu," *OC*, 2:315.

28. *"Les Mariés de la tour Eiffel,"* *Les Feuilles Libres,* February 1922, *OC*, 2:237.

29. "Ile-de-France, Ile d'Amour," *OC*, 2:338.

30. "La Règle du jeu," *OC*, 2:314.

31. "Ile-de-France, Ile d'Amour," *OC*, 2:332.

32. "The gaze of the symbolists, at certain hours, drowned in the sky; at other moments, in the absinth of the Montmartre bars. . . . Gazing rarely at the sky, I do not feel the need to imbibe." "Franc-Nohain," *OC*, 2:260–61. This article, published posthumously, was first sent as a chronicle/letter to Jacques Doucet in December 1919. There is irony in the references to drinking, in view of Radiguet's later heavy drinking.

33. "Depuis 1789, on me force à penser, j'en ai mal à la tête," *Le Coq,* May 1920, *OC*, 2:210–12.

34. "Jean Cocteau," letter/chronicle to Jacques Doucet (December 1919), *OC*, 2:259.

. 35. Ibid., p. 257.

36. *"Parade,"* *Le Gaulois,* December 25, 1920, *OC*, 2:222.

37. "Conseils aux grands poetes" (Advice to great poets), *Le Coq,* November 1920, *OC*, 2:218.

38. "Ingres et le cubisme," *Le Gaulois,* May 21, 1921, *OC*, 2:223–26.

39. Malcolm Haslam, *The Real World of the Surrealists* (New York: Rizzoli, 1978), p. 31.

40. "Notes sur la droite et la gauche littéraires," (Notes on the literary right and left), in *Désordre, OC,* 2:379.

41. Nolte, *Three Faces of Fascism,* p. 103.

42. Ibid., p. 66. Maurras also used the slogan "France first!" (p. 105).

43. Stressing Maurras's consistency and love of order, Malraux wrote a "Notice" for Maurras's *Mlle Monk,* a series of essays on the nineteenth century (Paris; reprint, 1923).

44. Maurras, *Critique et Poésie,* p. 189.

45. "Notes sur la droite et la gauche littéraires," *OC,* 2:379.

46. Ibid., pp. 379–80.

47. "Notes critiques diverses," *OC,* 2:382.

48. Ibid., "stupide dix-neuvième siècle," p. 382. Léon Daudet, *Le Stupide XIXe siècle* (Paris: Nouvelle Librairie Nationale, 1922), described in Nolte, *Three Faces of Fascism,* p. 473.

49. "Return to Louis 14—subsidies to newspapers—the press is dying—literature will rise again—Its influence on opinion." "Notes sur la droite et la gauche littéraires," *OC*, 2:380.

50. "Notes critiques diverses," *OC*, 2:383.

51. Ibid.

52. "Début d'un journal," *OC*, 2:399. Radiguet protested against Cocteau's describing the Middle Ages as an "age of darkness." Radiguet's journal, begun in August 1923, was inspired by that of Jean Hugo but was not kept beyond the first few days. Radiguet, like Maurras, made little distinction between Middle Ages and Renaissance, seeing rather the continuity that links the two eras.

53. Nolte, *Three Faces of Fascism*, p. 72.

54. "Début d'un journal," *OC*, 2:400.

55. "Ile-de-France, Ile d'Amour, *OC*, 2:339–40.

56. Ibid., pp. 337–38.

57. Ibid., p. 338.

58. "Début d'un journal," *OC*, 2:400.

59. "Notes sur la droite et la gauche littéraires," *OC*, 2:378.

Chapter Six

1. Salmon, *Souvenirs sans fin*, 1:187.

2. Ibid., 2:42.

3. Roger Nimier, *Journées de lecture* (Paris: Gallimard, 1965), p. 235.

4. Arthur Rimbaud, letter to Georges Izambard, August 25, 1870, in *Oeuvres Complètes* (Paris: Gallimard, 1972), p. 238.

5. "Ile-de-France, Ile d'Amour," *OC*, 2:327.

6. Maurice Martin du Gard, *Les Mémorables* (Paris: Flammarion, 1957), p. 208.

7. "La Règle du jeu," *OC*, 2:314.

8. *Désordre, OC*, 2:371: "Et pour être heureux paraît-il / Il ne faut pas songer au paradis / Mais moi j'y pense sans remords / Quand je suis né, il était mort." *Désordre* is the title given by Simone Lamblin to a miscellaneous collection of unpublished peices found after Radiguet's death.

9. Martin du Gard, *Les Mémorables*, p. 335, quoting Gide.

10. Jacques Porel, *Fils de Réjane* (Son of Rejane) (Paris: Plon, 1951), 1:352–53.

11. Guillaume Apollinaire, "Zone," in *Alcools. Oeuvres Poétiques* (Paris: Gallimard, 1956), p. 116: "Tu lis les prospectus les catalogues les affiches qui chantent tout haut / Voilà la poésie ce matin et pour la prose il y a les journaux / Il y a les livraisons à 25 centimes pleines d'aventures policières / . . . . / J'ai vu ce matin une jolie rue dont j'ai oublié le nom / . . . . / Le matin par trois fois la sirène y gémit / Une cloche rageuse y

aboie vers midi / Les inscriptions des enseignes et des murailles / Les plaques les avis à la facon des perroquets criaillent / J'aime la grâce de cette rue industrielle."

12. Jacques Rivière, in *N.R.F.*, June 1924, p. 692.

13. Albert Thibaudet, in *N.R.F.*, July 1924, p. 196.

14. The doubt as to whether Radiguet was man or boy persisted. He was buried in a white casket, that of a child; but the invitation to the funeral qualified him as a "man of letters." The white coffin was controversial.

15. Jean Cocteau, *Entretiens avec André Fraigneau* (Paris: Seuil, 1965), pp. 36–37.

16. Ibid., p. 2.

17. *Un Pauvre Homme, projet de roman* (A poor man, project for a novel). These notes, which of course never led to a completed novel, are in *Désordre, OC*, 2:384–85.

18. Ibid., p. 388.

Selected Bibliography

PRIMARY SOURCES

Neither set of *Oeuvres Complètes* is truly complete, although the two volumes edited by Simone Lamblin contain poems, drafts, notes, and critical articles missing from the single-volume *Oeuvres Complètes* published by Grasset and reprinted by Slatkine. It is the Slatkine, however, that is readily available, whereas the Lamblin edition is not.

Le Bal du comte d'Orgel. Preface by Jean Cocteau. Paris: Bernard Grasset, 1924 (Gallimard, Collection "Folio," 1983).
Le Diable au corps. Paris: Bernard Grasset, 1923 (Gallimard, Collection "Folio," 1982).
Les Joues en feu et autres poèmes. Paris: Tchou, 1967.
Les Joues en feu. Edited by Jean-Louis Major. Ottawa: Editions de l'Université, 1977.
Oeuvres Complètes. Paris: Grasset, 1952 (Slatkine, Collection "Ressources," 1981).
Oeuvres Complètes. 2 vols. Edited by Simone Lamblin. Paris: Club des Libraires de France, 1959.

English translations:
Ball at Count d'Orgel's. Translated by Malcolm Cowley. New York: Norton, 1929.
Cheeks on Fire, Collected Poems. Translated by Alan Stone. London: John Calder, 1976; New York: Riverrun, 1980.
Count d'Orgel Opens the Ball. Translated by Violet Schiff. London: Harvill, 1952. Under the title *Count d'Orgel,* New York: Grove, 1970.
Devil in the Flesh. Translated by Kay Boyle. Introduction by Aldous Huxley. Paris: Black Sun Press, 1932; New American Library, Signet Books, 6th ed. 1955.
The Devil in the Flesh. Translated by Alan Sheridan Smith. London: Calder and Boyars, 1971.
The Pelicans. In *Modern French Plays.* Edited by Michael Benedikt and George E. Wellworth. New York: Faber, 1975.

SECONDARY SOURCES

Boillat, Gabriel. *Un Maître de 17 ans, Raymond Radiguet.* Neuchâtel: la Baconnière, 1973. An unusual study, of the commercial and publication record of the novels, with important information on Radiguet's relations with Bernard Grasset, his publisher.

Borgal, Clément. *Radiguet.* Paris: Editions Universitaires, "Classiques du XXᵉ Siècle," 1969. A useful general introduction to Radiguet, it points out Radiguet's debt as a poet to his predecessors.

Bouraoui, H. A. "Radiguet's *Le Diable au corps:* Beneath the Glass Cage of Form." *Modern Language Quarterly* 34 (March 1973):64–77. The narrator is presented as attempting to make his life into an artistic creation.

Chanel, Pierre, ed. "Raymond Radiguet, Jean Cocteau." *Cahiers Jean Cocteau* 4 (1973). An invaluable special issue on Radiguet. A. Oliver convincingly shows Cocteau's preponderant role in preparing *Le Bal* for publication: in effect a rewriting. Oliver announces impending publication of a critical edition of *Le Bal.* To date it has not appeared. Other articles on *Le Diable* and the work at large, and previously unpublished letters and minor pieces.

Crosland, Margaret. *Raymond Radiguet: A Biographical Study with Selections from His Work.* London: Peter Owen, 1976. A useful introduction to shorter texts by Radiguet, arranged chronologically. Draws heavily upon biographers Odouard and Steegmuller.

Dieudonné, Serge. "Cocteau entre soi-même et Radiguet." *Cahiers Jean Cocteau* 8 (1979):193–206. Good analysis of the poetry, and of the unique character of Radiguet's friendship with Cocteau.

Garuti delli Ponti, Liliana. *Gli Inediti.* Parma: Guanda, 1967. Has an informative preface by Luigi de Nardis and a number of unpublished pieces, including the joint venture *Paul et Virginie,* and the erotic poetry *Vers Libres.*

Goesch, Keith. *Raymond Radiguet, étude biographique.* Paris-Geneva: La Palatine, 1955. First full-length book on Radiguet, it remains a worthwhile starting point for a study of the author.

Milorad. "Romans-jumeaux ou de l'imitation." *Cahiers Jean Cocteau* 8 (1979):87–107. Successfully demonstrates Radiguet's influence on Cocteau in the writing of novels.

Noakes, David. *Raymond Radiguet.* Paris: Seghers, Collection "Poètes d'aujourd'hui," 181, 1952; nouvelle édition, 1968. Still the most careful and enlightening introduction to the poetry of Radiguet.

Odouard, Nadia. *Les Années Folles de Raymond Radiguet*. Paris: Seghers, "L'Archipel," 1974. Examines love in Radiguet's life and novels. Especially useful for appendixes containing previously unpublished correspondence, manuscript variants, and poems.

Oliver, Andrew. See "Chanel" above.

—————. "Le Bal du comte d'Orgel, structure, mythe, signification." *Revue des Langues Modernes* 81, fasc. 1 (1975):109–20, and 82, fasc. 1, no. 2 (1977):161–84. Perhaps the most penetrating analysis of *Le Bal* to have appeared, it charts an archetypal pattern of initiation.

Pérébinossoff, Philippe R. "Amusement and Control: The Theatricals of Raymond Radiguet's *Count d'Orgel*." *Romance Notes* 17, no. 1 (Fall 1976):131–36. Sees all of the characters in *Le Bal* as affected by Anne's identity as impresario. Neglects importance of Anne's heredity.

Senninger-Book, Claude-Marie. "*Le Bal du Comte d'Orgel*, une *Princesse de Clèves* du vingtième siècle." Symposium 17, no. 2 (Summer 1963):130–143. A useful examination of Radiguet's borrowings from Mme de La Fayette in the composition of his second novel.

Steegmuller, Francis. *Cocteau: A Biography*. Boston: Little, Brown, 1970. This exemplary biography is fair and complete in its treatment of Cocteau—a unique achievement—and invaluable in its charting of his relations with Radiguet.

Turnell, Martin. "Raymond Radiguet, the Infant Prodigy." *Southern Review* 11, no. 3 (July 1975):553–76. Although apparently influenced by Odouard, quite a useful guide to Radiguet's life and his novels. Weak on the poetry.

Index

DATE DUE

GAYLORD			PRINTED IN U.S.A.